THE
BOOK
BIBLE

**HOW TO SELL YOUR MANUSCRIPT—NO MATTER
WHAT GENRE—WITHOUT GOING BROKE OR INSANE**

SUSAN SHAPIRO

Foreword by Ayesha Pande

Skyhorse Publishing

Skyhorse Publishing books may be purchased in bulk at special discounts for sales promotion, corporate gifts, fund-raising, or educational purposes. Special editions can also be created to specifications. For details, contact the Special Sales Department, Skyhorse Publishing, 307 West 36th Street, 11th Floor, New York, NY 10018 or info@skyhorsepublishing.com.

Skyhorse® and Skyhorse Publishing® are registered trademarks of Skyhorse Publishing, Inc.®, a Delaware corporation.

Visit our website at www.skyhorsepublishing.com.

10 9 8 7 6 5 4 3 2

Library of Congress Cataloging-in-Publication Data is available on file.

Cover design by Eyal Solomon
Cover art by Ron Agam

ISBN: 978-1-5107-6270-1
E-book ISBN: 978-1-5107-6369-2

Printed in the United States of America

To the wonderful, generous, amazing Mickey Shapiro,
who is really sick of book events

Table of Contents

Foreword by Ayesha Pande   vii
Introduction   xi

SECTION 1: NONFICTION   **1**
Chapter 1: Memoir/Autobiography   3
Chapter 2: Biographies   25
Chapter 3: How-To Books/Self-Help   38
Chapter 4: Nonfiction Book Proposals   49

SECTION 2: SHORTER BOOKS   **79**
Chapter 5: Poetry   81
Chapter 6: Anthologizing   91
Chapter 7: Humor and Graphics   103

SECTION 3: FICTIONALIZING   **111**
Chapter 8: Adult Fiction   113
Chapter 9: Genre Fiction   132

SECTION 4: CHILDREN'S LIT   **145**
Chapter 10: Picture Books   147
Chapter 11: Middle-Grade   156
Chapter 12: Young Adult   166

SECTION 5: SELLING YOUR BOOK   **177**
Chapter 13: Figuring Out Genre   179
Chapter 14: Querying Literary Agents   188

Glossary   202
Acknowledgments   209
About the Author   211
Index   212

Foreword

BY AYESHA PANDE

On a good day as a longtime agent, I feel like a modern fairy godmother who makes literary dreams come true. Yet it takes more than waving a glittery wand to create a book. Luckily, this essential guide by my colleague Susan Shapiro illuminates all the work behind the wizardry. Susan, a bestselling author and acclaimed professor, provides invaluable insider knowledge and concrete steps to help aspiring authors launch their words into the world.

We first met fifteen years ago, right after I'd opened my Harlem-based boutique literary agency. Susan heard I was seeking new authors whose voices didn't get enough play in the publishing industry.

"Boy, do I have an audience who needs you," she said.

She invited me to join her popular panels of experts at The New School, NYU and Columbia University to share what I'd learned as an agent and former editor. The large crowds were filled with aspiring authors of every ethnicity, religion, career and background, from seventeen-year-old undergraduates to retired seniors. Insanely excited about publishing, they seemed especially inspired to hear that I championed under-represented writers. Many asked about my clients, like the lyrical novelists Patricia Engel and Lisa Ko, award-winning short story writer Danielle Evans, and activist scholar Ibram X. Kendi, author of the National Book Award–winning nonfiction books *Stamped* and the revelatory blockbuster *How to Be an Anti-Racist*.

My fascination for eclectic, unsung stories is not surprising since I grew up as a biracial émigré with divorced parents, moving between India, Germany and New Zealand before coming to the United States. As I was an outsider wherever we lived, books were my constant friend, escape, addiction and therapy. Even though my adventurous German mother always pushed me to go outside to climb trees or hike in the woods, I preferred to stay under the covers with Robert Louis Stevenson's *Treasure Island* or Astrid Lindgren's *Pippi Longstocking*.

After high school in Wellington, New Zealand, I moved to Calcutta to live with my father, a Bengali who could recite hundreds of poems by Wordsworth and T.S. Eliot. He inspired in me an enduring love for British authors like Thomas Hardy, Aldous Huxley and George Orwell. (How telling that a brown Englishman focused on the white male canon while neglecting the brilliant literature to be found in his native Bengal.) After he died, I was touched to find a secret cache of his own poetry hidden among his papers.

Unlike Susan, I didn't study English or writing. My degrees were in history and international affairs from Washington and Columbia Universities, because if I couldn't be a doctor, my Asian dad decided I should work in foreign affairs. Instead of landing at the United Nations, I applied my diplomatic skills as an editor at Farrar Straus, HarperCollins and Crown Publishers before founding my literary agency, where my heart and brain were immersed in shepherding important fiction and nonfiction into the universe (along with my two wonderful children).

During the age of self-publishing, when indie and online editors can be contacted directly, Susan often asks me to discuss why a writer may need someone like me to handle their business affairs. Now more than ever it's smart to have a professional representing work on your behalf. As Susan explains in her chapter on approaching agents, we're a mix of editor, teacher, salesperson, career coach, therapist, matchmaker, manager and cheerleader. When we take on a client, we become the

The Book Bible

author's team, protector and advocate, helping them navigate the publishing realm, read contracts and get the best deals, often for their entire careers. The eight employees at my agency have handled authors from age twenty-one to seventy-five working as actors, academics, historians, editors, activists, parents, veterans and students—who usually receive advances between $300 and $300,000 and sometimes even more.

Not that it's easy to land a good agent or editor. It helps when you have an extraordinary teacher like Susan, whose students have sold impressive books in all genres. At Susan's events, fellow agents, editors and new authors share such tips as: take writing classes with an author you want to emulate, start a weekly criticism workshop with tough critics, or hire a ghost editor for guidance. Yet for people who can't be at these fun and electrifying panels, or afford the time, money or commitment to get a degree or pay for outside editorial assistance, *The Book Bible* contains everything you need to know about what to do—and what not to do.

"What would make you reject an author out of hand?" is a question Susan frequently begs me to address, to keep her students from making mistakes that lead to rejection.

In the spirit of her "instant gratification takes too long" philosophy, I explain how my agency gets hundreds of submissions; I can receive forty a day myself, so I have to be discerning. Unfortunately, I often get queries where someone offers their "fiction novel," "fictionalized memoir," "sci-fi poems," or "2,000-page masterpiece." That automatically telegraphs that the sender is unfamiliar with the terms used to categorize books, hasn't checked my website requirements or done their homework. By the time you're ready to query an agent, there's no excuse to not learn the basics of the industry. Yet it's hard to know which expert to trust. Many guides focus only on how to write a novel or a memoir, without even defining the terminology. *The Book Bible* is the one inclusive reference I've seen that spans twenty genres, delineates the idiosyncratic differences between categories, and sheds light on both the craft *and* the business of being an author. Susan teaches you how to research which kind of project you're imagining or pitching, as well as the most incisive ways to meet your goal.

The secret weapon she tells her protégés, based on her own experience, is to sell a short piece related to their book in an impressive place like the *New York Times, Washington Post, Wall Street Journal* or *The New Yorker* to speed up the slow publishing process. It's excellent advice because if I see an intriguing article, essay or op-ed, I often contact the author myself. That happened with an impressive piece I read in *BuzzFeed* by Christine Hyung-Oak Lee on the debilitating stroke she suffered at thirty-three. It led to a two-book deal for her evocative memoir *Tell Me Everything You Don't Remember* and an upcoming novel.

Miraculously, despite wild economic ups and downs and frequent dire predictions of demise, literature has proved timeless and enduring. Even at the start of the pandemic, book deals kept happening daily and I sold a debut novel, crime fiction by Aamina Ahmad, to Penguin Random House. It's the most exhilarating feeling when a great editor says yes and I get to call my author to share the magic words: "Your book will be published." They'll cry and scream, and then send chocolate, cookies or flowers. Many times I'm screaming and crying too!

I'm grateful to be able to play a small part enhancing the culture by reshaping the literary landscape. It's an honor to contribute to this smart, soulful guide by a fellow book lover dedicated to helping new authors find their path and passion. Just make sure to read it *before* you pitch any editors or agents.

Introduction

It's hard to make a living as a writer, yet 81 percent of people in this country want to be authors, according to *American Scholar* editor Joseph Epstein. After the excitement of publishing more than a dozen books myself, and the vicarious thrill of helping students sell hundreds of projects, I'm surprised the number isn't higher. But like the luminary Ayesha Pande, I've always been book obsessed.

When my third-grade teacher distributed catalogues of paperback humor, science, poetry, history and novels, I wanted them all. My Midwest parents gave me ten bucks. Spotting a few fives in the kitchen drawer, I swiped those too. While classmates each picked a few, I was the high roller who bought every title. I later feared the theft was a sign of my privilege and immorality. Yet in retrospect, it also forecasted my career as a prolific author and writing teacher celebrating students with hardcovers in every section of the bookstore. After all, nobody hands you a byline or a book with your name on it. You have to be hungry, determined and desperate enough to grab it.

Are *you*?

"If you want to be a writer, you must do two things above all else," advised Stephen King. "Read a lot and write a lot." While it helps to be reading exactly what you want to be writing, I always tried to read everything. By high school, I was devouring a mix of highbrow and low: *Cosmopolitan,* Sylvia Plath's *Ariel,* Maya Angelou's *I Know Why the Caged Bird Sings,* Philip Roth's *Portnoy's Complaint* and Dale Carnegie's *How to Win Friends and Influence People,* plus my parents' *Detroit News, Free Press, New York Times* and *Wall Street Journal.* A teacher told me: hang out with people you want to be. Listening, I applied to graduate writing programs.

At twenty-two, finishing my degree at NYU and selling my first piece to *Cosmo,* I ran twenty blocks in heels to buy up the newsstand copies. I wound up with bylines in all those newspapers my folks subscribed to (a great place to begin), then on the covers of poetry, fiction, memoir and self-help books. Still, it took forever to afford my rent, even moonlighting as a teacher.

In twenty-five years at The New School and New York University, I've shared all my past errors to keep the people in my classes from repeating my mistakes and waiting until middle age to figure it out, like I did. I feared my penchant for switching categories made me seem like a dabbler. But now I see my versatility has an upside. Over the last decade I've helped students publish more than 150 books in all genres, earning advances between $1,000 and $500,000. Though the literary world feels like a secret society, it's not. Publishers are desperate for hot debut authors—if you learn the inside scoop that I'm sharing to break in.

Of course, it's much easier to publish 3 pages than 300. Selling a short piece in a top place is the best way to get an agent or editor to contact you. My first guide, *The Byline Bible,* shows how writing can turn your worst experiences into the most beautiful, as well as lucrative. Former students' op-eds and personal essays on addiction, mental illness, infertility, military service, divorce, immigration and racism expanded into books. Everyone wants to know how they did it. *The Book Bible* tells you.

Here I map out the details of different kinds of projects that top editors want, along with writing, revising and marketing strategies, offering a clear plan to authorship. I share my bias towards work sold through agencies like Ayesha's, since that was my path to success. While there are already some good instruction manuals out there, none cover all the categories and steps, from crafting plot to querying agents to launching and publicity.

"Some people say publishing is a business, but it's really a casino," the late Daniel Menaker, former executive editor in chief of Random House, once told me. Still, there are ways to improve your odds with knowledge I wish I had earlier in my career:

> Which genres usually require a full manuscript to sell to an editor? (Fiction and poetry.) Which category is easiest to sell to a publisher with the fewest pages? (Nonfiction.) Must I be famous to get a book deal for a memoir? (No, but you need a great story.) If I want a decent advance, should I get an agent or go directly to publishers? (Agent.) Will my book be fact-checked? (Probably not; the onus is on you.) Do you recommend self-publishing? (No, though there are times when it makes sense.)

I could have used this overview while studying English at the University of Michigan and creative writing at NYU. My impressive instructors assigned their own acclaimed books, yet never offered names of editors or agents. It was verboten to ask. They offered no publishing courses for aspiring authors or ways to navigate this bumpy journey, ignoring the business side that blinded me. In fine arts degrees, the focus is still more process than profession, barely mentioning student internships, jobs or freelance opportunities to pay tuition or debt. I've taught in MFA programs that cost $70,000 annually, as much as an MD, JD or MBA. I love when students say they learned more about publishing in my two-hour seminar than in all of undergrad and grad school combined. To paraphrase Mark Strand: I became what was missing.

In college, poems I spent four years on were accepted by literary journals that only paid in copies. A favorite instructor I hounded recommended me for a minimum wage editorial assistant job at *The New Yorker*, proving that the squeaky wheel does indeed get the grease. The magazine paid me $1,200 for a profile of a man who collected meteorites, but my editor left and it ended up running elsewhere. A fellow assistant hooked me up with her *Cosmopolitan* editor friend who bought and ran my amusing "Outrageous Opinion" breakup humor pieces for $500 each—until they nixed that column. I switched from frustrated poet and not-hilarious-enough humorist to overeager *New York Times Book Review* critic. Assignments paid $100 plus a free book.

In another absurdly non-lucrative turn, after years of struggling, at twenty-nine I became *Newsday's* paperback columnist for $300 weekly. But I could choose what I reviewed, a rare perk. I devoured books one hundred hours a week, while on buses, subways, at my local diner and doing leg lifts in exercise class. At lunch someone asked, "You have little kids at home?" He pointed to the chicken I'd cut into small pieces, my habit so I could turn pages faster. Fat packages of books came to my apartment—every day was Hanukkah! On a trip to Jamaica with my boyfriend, I brought more books than bathing suits. Was that why he dumped me for an actress?

Depressed, I admitted to my editor that critiquing twenty books a month burned me out, hoping he'd reduce it to four. He reduced it to zero, replacing me with another poetry MFA (poets work cheap) who only had to do three reviews weekly. "Both my lover and editor dumped me for other women," I told my shrink. "Which is worse, my ex with a younger girl, or my byline replaced by a better poet? I can't envision any job I'll like as much as being a critic with my own column."

"Didn't you say you really wanted to write your own books?" she asked.

If you can afford a good shrink, you won't regret it. Mine danced at both my book party and wedding. But it was easier to land a husband than a hardcover. A comic novel I tried was rejected by thirty agents. I didn't know not to send out an early draft, since you only get one shot. Asking advice from mentors is a good move. Mine said, "You have no imagination whatsoever. Try nonfiction." An editor at Berkeley Press who liked my *Cosmo* humor asked me to do a relationship humor guide.

But I didn't realize signing a contract directly with a publisher could be to my disadvantage, as agents often negotiate higher advances and royalties. In the chapter on how to find literary representation, you'll learn why it's better to figure it out before your debut.

My little paperback *The Male-to-Female Dictionary* came out when I was thirty-five, the same year I married a hilarious scriptwriter. And I found a tiny publisher for my poetry manuscript. It sold a grand total of about 20 copies, mostly to me and my relatives. A mentor gave me a blurb praising the book, but privately admitted, "You have too many words, not enough music."

Crushed, I took a job as an adjunct professor. (I advise aspiring writers to find day jobs or side hustles, since my teaching salary made my books possible.) The first assignment I gave my students: write 3 pages on your most humiliating secret. This is the prompt that has led to the most publications ever. (Try it.) When several pieces they published led to hardcover deals, I felt like the wedding planner who couldn't wed. So I took my own advice to mine my indignities. Besides my ex who left me for the actress, other embarrassing breakups from my past haunted me. "If you got the story tell it; if you ain't got it, write it," a mentor said. Since I hadn't fought in war or solved world hunger, I at least found a universally intriguing conceit. What if I visited my top five heartbreakers, asking what really went wrong? As Nora Ephron said, "Everything is copy."

I crafted a proposal for my comical nonfiction sex, drugs, breakup and marriage memoir, not knowing that debut memoirs (like novels) often require a completed manuscript. Agents said, "It's funny, but there's not enough here." To prove them wrong, I wrote 225 pages. Debating whether to call it fiction or nonfiction, an editor friend said, "A novel that is merely autobiographical is a great disappointment, but a memoir that reads like a novel is a great surprise." I used an "Author's Note" to explain my narrative strategy: "Names, dates, and personal characteristics have been changed for literary cohesion, to protect privacy and so my husband won't divorce me." I spent $2,500 for a ghost editor who kicked it into shape. "You have to spend money to make money" was true for me. It was a good investment, since the book sold for twenty times the editing expenditure, though I'll also share ways to minimize your financial risk while maximizing your advance.

At forty-three, when my first hardcover memoir *Five Men Who Broke My Heart* came out, someone asked how long it took. "Twenty-three years of banging my head against the wall, then six months," I said. When *New York Times* and *The Oprah Magazine* critics called my book frank, funny and "a mind-bendingly good read," I yelled, "This is the happiest moment of my life!"

"Not our wedding day?" my husband asked.

"I adore you," I said. "But any dummy can wed. You just need another dummy. Not everybody can sell a book."

Writers often pick a lane, labelling themselves a "poet," "novelist," "short story writer," "memoirist" or "biographer." I just say "author." If a project is rejected, I reinvent myself, revise my pages and try a new category. To do this, you first have to understand the different classifications, knowing, for example, that nonfiction must be true and there's no such thing as a YA/memoir/historical fantasy hybrid. Editors say, "Don't write for the market, write for love," and "Finish the book first, then figure out what it is." Still, it's smart to decide early on which bookstore shelf your project will fit. When an undergrad asked me to read his 700-page sci-fi thriller in rhyming iambic pentameter, I said, "Don't invent your own genre. Learn the categories and rules before you break them." Students try timely ideas that are trending. Yet mainstream books can take years from "yes" to completion. By the time you jump on a trend, it may be over.

Genre can be fluid though, if you're flexible. A nonfiction draft turned into a splashy novel and led to selling my first attempt at fiction thirteen years after I started. (Instead of a book launch, it got a Book Mitzvah.) When I tried the memoir *Secrets of a Fix-Up Fanatic*, about being set up by a mutual friend as well as fixing up thirty couples as an amateur matchmaker, I was told it was boring. Turning it into self-help with the subtitle "How to Meet and Marry Your Match" made it fly—especially after I guest starred on a reality TV dating show as the love guru. Someone who took my seminar did a radio interview that led her to a six-figure two-book deal. Getting press or going viral on social media helps a book sell faster—another trick I'll unpack.

My eclectic oeuvre now includes several memoirs (one coauthored), three novels (two comic, one indie), an anthology, self-help books, middle-grade fiction and the pop culture chronicle of Barbie for a coffee table tome. Who knew being a low-end doll collector, amateur match-maker, former addict and rejected lover would be perfect platforms for books? As I advise my students: "Explore your worst obsessions."

What's yours? Try writing about it.

Here's what not to do: A man from Australia emailed "I'll be in New York Sunday. Can I take you to lunch to pick your brain about how to sell my book?" A Texas colleague called to ask, "Would you read my novel and recommend your agent?" Similar queries motivated script-writer Josh Olson's hilarious *Village Voice* piece "I Will Not Read Your Fucking Script." He ranted, "If that seems unfair, I'll make you a deal: In return for you not asking me to read your fucking script, I will not ask you to wash my fucking car, or take my fucking picture, or represent me in fucking court, or take out my fucking gall bladder, or whatever the fuck it is that *you* do for a living."

I loved his sublime response. Yet as a teacher who enjoys inspiring people, I never want to say, "I'm too busy writing my own book. Why don't you take my online class?" Now I can be cheerful and helpful by saying the words every successful author must learn: "Here's a link to buy my book." It's a sentiment you'll appreciate more after you sign a contract to get yours published.

SECTION ONE:
NONFICTION

CHAPTER 1

Memoir/Autobiography

HOW TO ENSURE YOUR FIRST-PERSON NONFICTION WON'T BE PUBLISHED

1. **Refuse to Read Similar Books:** Write in a total vacuum. That way you'll delude yourself into thinking that your memoir on giving up the sauce, or your grandfather's death from cancer, is a brilliant, original idea that nobody has ever done before.

2. **Avoid All Writing Instruction:** Just wing it. You aced your college English papers twelve years ago and you've been successful in advertising. Even though you've spent decades in a completely different field, how hard could publishing a book be? Your words are golden, so make sure to rush out your first draft, no editing allowed.

3. **Be a Literary Snob:** Don't add a provocative title or subtitle, any topical updates, pop culture references, recent studies, a new perspective or a fresh spin to your old story. Geniuses should never have to compromise their artistic vision for crass marketing purposes (even if you're hoping for a six-figure advance from Random House).

4. **Pretend You're as Important as Presidents:** Narrate every single year you've lived for the sole reason that it really happened (even if it's mundane, confusing, irrelevant or tedious). Add a whole chapter about the time you shoved a raisin up your nose when you were

three and how you cried when meeting Santa Claus—since your grandma loves those stories.

5. **Trash Your Ex or Relatives You Hate:** Recite a litany of all the bad things your horrible ex, boss or mother did to you to get revenge in print. Play victim, forgetting to mention that your own neurosis, alcoholism or drug abuse contributed in any way to your being busted, broke or alone. Use real names, professions and identifying characteristics, making it so nasty that your work is libelous and you get sued. No publicity is bad publicity, right?

6. **Try to Sell a Book of Your Previously Published Work:** Bestselling authors Janet Malcolm and Ian Frazier got book-length collections from their magazine pieces. No matter that their great pieces first debuted to great acclaim in *The New Yorker*. Your personal essays got 1,000 claps on Medium—same thing, no?

7. **Stay Light and Breezy:** Avoid any pain or deep revelations. The world is depressing enough, you don't have to add to it. Tina Fey's memoir was funny, so figure yours can be too. Forget that her book sold well because she's Tina Fey, with millions of fans from *Saturday Night Live*, *Mean Girls* and *30 Rock*.

8. **Lie Through Your Teeth:** You need to be more dramatic, so what's a few fibs? Don't tell your agent or editor the true story, so they get ambushed by the fallout when a critic realizes—a la James Frey on *Oprah*—you've passed off fiction as nonfiction.

9. **Plagiarize Others and Yourself:** Google information that you include from other sources with no citations or indications that the sentences you are quoting aren't your own. Nobody will notice if you paraphrase Wikipedia, will they? Also be sure to repeat what you've already published, without mentioning it's from your earlier work, assuming it'll be a good way to build a new audience.

10. **Expect Immediate Success:** Be impatient, entitled and bitter when literary agents you've never met don't get back to you within a month. Then tell everyone, "See? It's impossible to break into publishing," ignoring the thousands of memoirs that come out every

year by authors who worked harder, revised longer and exercised more patience and respect for the written word.

BETTER WAYS TO CRAFT YOUR OWN STORY

"I'm tired, everybody's tired of my turmoil," wrote Robert Lowell.

Actually, we're not. A half century after his death, we're still buying his books about his struggles with family, divorce and manic depression. Although he mostly crafted poignant poems from his personal chaos, he also published essays, plays, translations and criticism. His Pulitzer Prize and other awards confirmed that confessional poets were onto something: revealing your own drama/conflict/tension can be fascinating. Maybe that's why major wordsmiths like Vladimir Nabokov, Mary Karr, Maya Angelou, Gregory Orr and Donald Hall crossed genres to publish memoirs.

Although poetry, essay collections, novels, short fiction and self-help can delve into explorations of intimate experiences, each category has its own rules and expectations. Autobiography, as it used to be called, is the written history of the author's entire life, told from their perspective, using "I." Memoir, as it is now referred to, is usually a revealing chronicle that focuses on someone's most fascinating, dramatic personal experience. It can revolve around a time, place, job, class, experience, hobby or specific relationship.

First-person books are wildly popular, often topping the charts, even in a bad economy. The biggest advances go to the biggest celebrities like Bruce Springsteen, Shaquille O'Neal and Sally Field, who used the old autobiographical model, detailing their childhoods through their successful careers. Amy Schumer, Steve Martin, Mindy Kaling, Issa Rae, Eddie Huang and Rachel Dratch offered more light-hearted idiosyncratic humor. Bestseller lists are filled with books by political figures like the Obamas, Clintons, Bushes and Sonya Sotomayor. With fifty books published, Jimmy Carter has made a cottage industry out of telling his life story. His book royalties clearly pay better than president-ing and peanut farming. Some famous people use ghostwriters; Michelle

Obama had the class to thank hers in the acknowledgments, which is actually good for all writers.

Happily for us, memoirs are not just for the rich and famous. The public is also hungry for passionate personal narratives from real people. The hits *Maid* by Stephanie Land, Tara Westover's *Educated*, J.D. Vance's *Hillbilly Elegy* and Reyna Grande's *A Dream Called Home* explore the authors' struggles with poverty, family and mental illness. If you haven't yet acquired a huge audience, you may have to be more cutting edge, centering on one specific topic in the news or area of popular interest. Acclaimed books in this category have covered addiction recovery, immigration, sex, gender and marital issues, overcoming medical traumas and psychoanalysis through the eyes of a therapist in treatment herself. While you don't have to be an elected official, athlete or television star to sell your own personal narrative, you do need an important, focused, dramatic or engaging story that sheds light on a universal theme.

Yes, the sarcastic term "misery memoir" has been used to describe biographical literature concerned with triumph over personal trauma, illness, misfortune, failure or abuse, where something huge is at stake—often life itself. I can easily get engrossed in books of "pathography," as they are also called, so long as the darkness is balanced with humor or wisdom. I actually find the word "misery" can help writers understand what agents, editors and the public look for in this field: extremes. Think about your most humiliating secret. The worst thing that ever happened to you. The suffering you almost didn't survive.

Don't believe anyone who tells an aspiring author that quiet, silly, light or humorous memoirs are "in." (Make sure they aren't scammers charging hopeful writers lots of money to be featured in their online press.) There aren't many mainstream editors I know who will pay unknown, unpublished writers for muted, mundane little slices of life.

There's nothing meek about Elie Wiesel's Holocaust survival story *Night* which, since its 1960 publication, has sold 6 million copies (a haunting number, given the topic). Other award-winning classics of the genre include *Angela's Ashes* (Frank McCourt's cantankerous tale of his poor Irish childhood), Alison Bechdel's *Fun Home* (depicting her father's closeted homosexuality and suicide) and Dave Eggers' *A Heartbreaking Work of Staggering Genius* (which describes ways he took care of his younger brother after the loss of their parents). Roxane Gay's *Hunger* portrays how being gangraped in her teens led to extreme weight gain. These are brave, powerful voices that didn't feel a need to whisper.

I read as many memoirs as I could before pitching mine, which centered on my past substance abuse, self-destructive relationships and career and personal rejections. My Bosnian Muslim coauthor chronicled how he'd survived ethnic cleansing after his family was betrayed by their friends and neighbors. Former students have signed book deals on everything from their addiction and recovery to bipolar disorder, divorce, gender fluidity, scoliosis, sexual malfunctions, racism, homophobia and infertility. Here are ways your own experiences can get you paid and published.

To Write a Riveting Memoir:

1. **Determine Your Goal:** My family friend who survived World War II wanted a record of his life for his kids and grandchildren. My addiction specialist decided to gather decades of his work to help others overcome substance abuse. Do you hope to empower others who've suffered through divorce, rape, addiction, abortions, mental illness or racism? Some MFA graduates are most concerned with literary prestige. Many adult students take my classes hoping for money, acclaim, and to raise their platforms. Others want to get a better job—which explains the glut of hardcovers by presidential wannabes. Maybe you're committed to literary self-exploration since, as Joan Didion says, "I write entirely to find out what I'm thinking." There are artistic, academic, indie, commercial, online, self-help and pay-as-you-go presses. Since each aim may lead you

to a different kind of publisher, I'd start by figuring out your end game.

2. **Get Classy:** You wouldn't assume you could be a doctor or lawyer without credentials, yet many people think they can be an author quickly on their own. If you're not having luck getting published, there are ways to learn to perfect your craft. Tons of impressive books have come out of the writing programs where I've taught at The New School, NYU and Columbia University. While they don't emphasize the business side, they can definitely help you improve your work. If you're a beginner, consider getting a four-year undergraduate English degree or a two-year MFA (and research options for scholarships and funding). For those who don't have the time or money, consider low-residency programs which can be cheaper, or take classes with authors whose work you admire, or former agents and editors who can give you tough criticism. Many talented memoirists teach shorter classes, seminars or summer workshops in person, at retreats and online, which allow you to keep your day job. Several students of mine sold their books after just one four-hour seminar.

If you can't take a class, at least do your homework. I once barged into an agent's office with my humorous carnal confessional *How to Stay Single Forever*. She went to her shelf and handed me a published book called *How to Stay Single Forever*. It hadn't occurred to me to check what had already hit the shelves. Before you start, research what's out there. Don't just Google or skim Amazon. Find a library, local or virtual bookstore to study the memoir shelves for subgenres. There are eyewitness political tomes, "my horrible childhood" confessions, addiction accounts, disastrous dating and mating narratives, medical dramas, domestic debacles, crime admissions, military exposés, sociological studies, pet sagas, food and travel memoirs, ethnic chronicles and leaving-your-religion tales. This will help you determine what your book is about and what subcategory it falls under. Then read the kind of books you want to be writing, which may give you permission, a plan and a template.

3. **Cultivate Your Voice:** While academic publishers prefer a studious tone and commercial presses might like more provocative inflections, you should still sound like yourself. If anybody else can tell your story, let them. Share what only you can write using your own rhythms, tonality and idiosyncratic speech. Some people enjoy polishing their storytelling techniques by talking into a microphone and transcribing later. Many students find it helpful to read their work aloud or journal every day. Try to keep other people's quotes to a minimum in your pages so you're not relying on someone else's words to convey your thoughts. Cut repetitions, get rid of clichés (like "tall, dark and handsome," "he's a bad egg," and "kiss and make up"). I often reread the poets Lucille Clifton, Joseph Brodsky, Yehuda Amichai, Rita Dove, Robert Lowell and Adrienne Rich. Their unusual phrasing and cadences remind me of the limitlessness of language. Study the voices of the writers you love to understand how they did it.

4. **Start Small:** It takes much less time to publish 3 pages than 300 and having a great clip can get agents and editors calling you. Try to sell a dramatic part of your memoir as a short essay in the *New York Times* Modern Love column, which editor Daniel Jones says has led to more than sixty book deals so far. Yes, it's a long shot, but I've made it in there twice, along with sixty of my students, five who have the column to thank for their books. Or you can aim for *The Wall Street Journal*, *The New Yorker*, *Washington Post*, *Slate*, *Salon*, *Newsweek*, NPR's *This American Life* or other publications that impress agents. My former student Aspen Matis's Modern Love piece about recovering from date rape, "A Hiker's Guide to Healing," led to the vice president of HarperCollins buying her memoir *Girl in the Woods*. Zack McDermott's Gawker piece "Mentally Unfit," about living with bipolarity, led to his memoir *Gorilla and the Bird*, which sold as an HBO mini-series. If no editor will publish your

essay, perhaps you're doing something wrong and need help. If you don't know where to start, mine your obsessions. When choosing a book topic, don't try one that will please your parents, spouse or professors, or a subject you think agents and editors will buy. Write what you find fascinating. What would *you* want to read, write and talk about for the next decade? A book can easily take five years to finish, and you might be promoting it long after that. So it better be a subject you could discuss forever. It doesn't have to be intellectual or the subject for a doctor of philosophy degree. Consider your pop culture idols, hobbies and neuroses. I was completely obsessed with Barbie dolls as a kid, bad breakups during my single years, stupid substance problems I was attempting to quit, how to make a living as a freelance writer, conquering my food addiction and my amateur matchmaking. Each of these became a book. Write a list of hobbies or obsessions you can explore.

5. **Find Your Tribe:** Before I finished my book projects, I benefitted from going to events and conventions hosted by The American Society for Journalists and Authors, Writers Digest, The Deadline Club, National Book Critics Circle, the Authors Guild of America, PEN American Center, The Jewish Book Council and the Brooklyn Book Festival. It was a way to meet agents and editors offering good advice. Colleagues across the country also recommend Publishing Triangle, Sisters in Crime, Poetry Society of America and Society of Children's Book Writers and Illustrators. There are specialized writing groups for Asians, veterans, Muslims, women, African and Native Americans, LGBTQ folk and Christian novelists, some with student discounts and scholarships. Colleges and bookstores offer free panels and lectures. If you can't get out, watch the twenty free videos of taped book talks on my website susanshapiro.net to hear advice from my favorite luminaries. They'll give you a sense of what editors and agents are looking for, which authors have exciting books out and how to position your own project in the future.

You should also explore social media possibilities. Some colleagues find it a headache to join Instagram, Snapchat, Tumblr, Reddit and other platforms. Yet as a freelancer, I stay up-to-date while expanding my audience. Young people in my classes sneer that Facebook, LinkedIn and Twitter are for old people. They forget that many executives on there are still the gatekeepers in publishing. So watch the photos of you getting stoned in an orgy, unless that's what your memoir is about and it's what you want to be known for. Follow editors and agents who sometimes put out calls for the type of work they want. (On Twitter I learned that a webzine edited by Roxane Gay paid a dollar a word for nonfiction.) I read two posts by students and commented, "take this off of Facebook, you can sell this," and the pieces ended up in the *L.A. Times* and *The Root*. A *Wall Street Journal* editor saw my post about anti-Semitism and bought a longer version for his op-ed section. Former students used their online exploits to launch books. Leandra Medine's *Man Repeller* blog turned into a book, online magazine and fashion phenomenon. *Granny Is My Wingman*, by Kayli Stollak, is a hardcover and TV pilot. Benjamin Grant told my class his hardcover *Overview* was launched with a few aerial photographs. It benefits you to see what's out there, stay connected and dip your toe into the public pool.

6. **Carve Out Time to Write:** Finishing a book can be a long trek and many people complain they don't have the time. But to get ahead, successful people do what others won't. When I had a full-time job for ten years, I wrote before work, on my commute, and at lunch, nights and weekends. At one position, I had an understanding boss who—if I finished all my tasks—would let me do my own thing. After I complained of writer's block, my bestselling cousin Howard Fast told me, "Plumbers don't get plumbers' block. Don't be self-indulgent, just get to work. A page a day is a book a year." That stayed with me. Now, no matter what else I have going on, I first type at least 250 words which is actually more than a book a year since

some of my books are around 200 pages. When busy students fear they can't finish a book while being parents with full-time jobs and commutes, I recall that the late poet Marie Ponsot, a mother of seven, published many books by writing in ten-minute segments. Think of short increments of time you can put to better use.

7. **Fight for Feedback:** It's rare that someone can stay home, finish a manuscript on their own, and sell it to a mainstream publisher. Writing is a collaborative process that benefits from outside perspective. As bestseller Stephen King advised: "Write with the door closed, rewrite with the door open." It's easy to get lost in the process of writing 200 or 300 pages. I loved workshopping my writing in an MFA program and subsequent classes. After that I found that bringing in pages to weekly writing workshops in my apartment keeps me motivated and gives me deadlines to bang it out. Others share sections of their book with one colleague who is crafting something similar. Some students I know use online forums to exchange work with like-minded scribes. Or you can hire a professional ghost editor like I've done. However you do it, it's smart to get tough criticism from an expert in the genre before you invest too many years of work. If you wait until you're on page 300, you might hear: wrong tense, your story is illogical, your hero comes across hateful. Find a system for getting critical notes while you are writing, lest you need to revise everything.

8. **Search for Your Niche:** Just because there are many books already on your topic doesn't mean there isn't room for yours. Yet you do have to find out exactly where you can add to the conversation. When I wanted to do my own addiction book I noticed there were tons of quitting alcohol, cocaine, crack and pill stories, but no funny first-person takes on getting rid of cigarettes and pot. Also every time I quit one substance, I'd get addicted to something else. Nobody had written about that, so I emphasized the phenomenon in my memoir *Lighting Up*. Cat Marnell's provocative bestseller

How to Murder Your Life shares her ambivalence about getting clean, offering a new twist to an old subject.

Make sure you're sharing your most compelling story. Unless you're an elected official, on a TV show or have a huge social media following, save the birth-to-death autobiography for your journal. For a mainstream publisher, prune your pages to the part of your life that would make a great, original memoir. If you were going to die in six months, what wisdom can you teach the world? For me, that came after a lot of therapy helped me end my self-destructive relationships. I revolved my first two memoirs around those topics (bad affairs, worse addictions). Even Barack Obama—a Harvard Law graduate with political ambitions—knew to center his 1995 debut memoir *Dreams From My Father* around his missing African dad and white mother. Ask yourself what happened to you that's unique, dramatic and fascinating.

9. **Take Twelve Months of Action:** People who've had a happy childhood may have to work harder to overcompensate, I joke to my classes. If you're young, grew up privileged, or don't yet have a compelling enough story, consider successful "stunt" memoirs, also called "immersion nonfiction," using a one-year adventure or game plan as a framework. Check out Gretchen Rubin's *The Happiness Project*, A.J. Jacob's *The Year of Living Biblically* and Shonda Rhimes' *The Year of Yes*. (Maria Dahvana Headley used that title too, in her debut memoir of saying yes to dating everyone nice who asked her out.) What could you do for a year or two that would warrant recording? Pick something you're dying to explore. Consider therapy or quitting an addiction through AA, NA or Weight Watchers, which could unblock you or teach you something. Travel or go on an investigative adventure like my colleague Tom Zoellner did in *Train: Riding the Rails That Created the Modern World from the Trans-Siberian to the Southwest Chief*. It might be something domestic, as in William Alexander's *52 Loaves,* about trying to rec-reate baking the perfect loaf of bread, as long as it's your passion.

Ann Patty learned Latin for *Living With a Dead Language;* Jhumpa Lahiri explored Italian in her memoir *In Other Words.* Take careful notes and photos so you can recreate your experiences. The word "author" is hidden in the word "authority"; become an expert so you'll have more to share with the world.

I'm jealous of the lucky authors who've had luck with a non-adventurous subcategory: sitting around reading and getting a book out of it. For these literary explorations, read a specific genre or author, take notes, and record surprising patterns or memories. Come up with a specific theory, argue for their importance or explore how your relationship to these books changed you. There's Wendy McClure's *The Wilder Life: My Adventures in the Lost World of Little House on the Prairie,* Andy Miller's *The Year of Reading Dangerously: How Fifty Great Books Saved My Life,* Lucy Mangan's *Bookworm: A Memoir of Childhood Reading,* Will Schwalbe's *Books for Living: Some Thoughts on Reading, Reflecting, and Embracing Life,* A.J. Jacobs's *The Know-It-All: One Man's Humble Quest to Become the Smartest Person in the World by reading the Encyclopedia Britannica from A to Z* and David L. Ulin's *The Lost Art of Reading: Why Books Matter in a Distracted Time.* Rebecca Mead's *My Life in Middlemarch* revisits the emotional connections she felt with George Eliot's classic. What new discovery or insights can you share?

10. **Package It:** While I applaud the desire to be chic, understated and subtle in real life, commercial success in memoirs rarely comes to introverts. (Unless that's what you're writing about, as in Jessica Pan's stunt memoir *Sorry I'm Late, I Didn't Want to Come: One Introvert's Year of Saying Yes.*) After decades of struggle with artsier titles, my breakout books were *Five Men Who Broke My Heart* and *Lighting Up: How I Stopped Smoking, Drinking and Everything Else I Loved in Life Except Sex.* I laughed at the titles for Chuck Klosterman's *Sex, Drugs, and Cocoa Puffs: A Low Culture Manifesto,* Jane Juska's *A Round-Heeled Woman: My Late-Life Adventures in Sex*

and Romance and Ophira Eisenberg's *Screw Everyone: Sleeping My Way to Monogamy.* Profanity has a history of selling too, as in Justin Halpern's *Sh*t My Dad Says*, Jen Agg's *I Hear She's a Real Bitch* and my friend Amy Alkon's *Good Manners for Nice People Who Sometimes Say F*ck.* I sometimes write a bunch of pages first, then steal my own best line for a title. I once used the headline an editor wrote for my book called *Secrets of a Fix-Up Fanatic* and someone in my weekly workshop (thanks Aspen!) came up with the title for my writing guide *Byline Bible*—a testament to the benefits of publishing short pieces and getting feedback from a weekly critique group.

While a pithy comic or provocative title is a good start, you need to sum up your book in a few lines, like a Hollywood movie pitch, a.k.a. "an elevator pitch." This is when you find a fast, sexy way to describe your project in case you get stuck in the elevator with Steven Spielberg who asks, "What's your book about?" I described *Five Men* as "a sex, drugs and marriage memoir about a woman who goes back to revisit her top five heartbreaks of all time to find out what really went wrong. A book for anyone who has ever wondered what happened to their first love. Or second. Or third. Or fourth. Or fifth . . . ." Before I showed an agent, I did a dedication page, made my own fantasy cover, had professional author's photos taken, asked well-known writers I knew for advance blurbs and printed it out so it looked like the book it became.

11. **Laser Focus:** When writing about yourself, it's easy to go off on long, winding tangents. That's why I often reread my title, subtitle and Hollywood movie pitch as I'm writing, to remind me exactly what this project has promised my readers and where I'm going. Sometimes I let myself run off in a different direction, then make a separate file for the meandering passages and return to my original narrative. Remember, if your first book does well, you may have the chance to publish another. I have three personal memoirs out. The late French feminist Simone de Beauvoir beat me with a four-edition autobiography, while the

Norwegian author Karl Ove Knausgård is on volume six. Work on one strand of your life at a time, saving anecdotes and detours for follow-up projects.

12. **Stop the Blame Game:** It's your story and you have a right to tell it. You usually don't need anybody's permission. Publishing lawyers will vet your manuscript for possible litigious passages. Yet your book can't read like an unabridged transcript of your therapy sessions. I don't know anyone who wants to read a sour-grapes kvetch about all the terrible things bad people did to you. Instead of writing a chronicle of your horrible parents, lovers, siblings, children or bosses, focus on how you recovered and turned it around. Jeanette Wall's *The Glass Castle*, *Them* by Francine du Plessix Gray, and Tara Westover's *Educated* are fine examples of how to show compassion for the relatives that failed you growing up. Still, make sure your memoir is mostly about you, and that you reveal, question, challenge and trash yourself more than anyone else.

    Either way, you can protect yourself by keeping proof of what you're writing. The late David Carr's triumphant heroin addiction memoir *The Night of the Gun* incorporates interviews he taped with former friends to get to the bottom of what really happened when he couldn't remember. His daughter Erin Lee Carr's poignant book about losing him, *All That You Leave Behind*, makes use of many of her father's emails. I save photographs and letters, tape interviews, and print out social media posts, cyber correspondence and tweets. It will help with fact-checking in the future and your publishing lawyer will be able to determine which names should be changed and who needs to sign release forms.

13. **Trace Your Arc:** Your memoir should not start and end in the same emotional place. Something has to change over the course of your book. As *Five Men* began, I was sure infertility would ruin my marriage and wondered if I'd chosen the wrong mate. It concluded (spoiler alert) with me realizing how much I loved my husband, regardless of whether we had a child. As *Lighting*

Up commenced, I had several ongoing addictions I couldn't quit. They were all gone by the last page. In *Bosnia List*, my coauthor Kenan Trebinčević felt sure his Muslim family was the most unfortunate in the Balkans during the ethnic cleansing campaign of 1993. Towards the end, he realized they were actually the luckiest since they'd all survived.

Sometimes before I get rolling, I write my first line and my last line just to make sure I'll have enough growth and character development. David Mamet, the famous dramatist, said that there are only three things an audience cares about: Who wants what from whom? What happens if they don't get it? Why now? Don't bog everything down with exposition and back story that dilutes the current action. Though film and TV's fictional formats are different than nonfiction books, to keep readers engaged, I make sure that I answer those three questions in every chapter and on every page. Though the crux of *The Bosnia List* is set during the Balkan War, my coauthor and I played up present-day friction as Kenan debates whether or not to go back and visit the homeland that exiled him because of his religion. We weaved Yugoslavian history into dialogue-filled scenes where he visits the cemetery to pay respects to his relatives buried there.

14. **Reveal Yourself:** What makes you impressive in real life (good looks, great job, gorgeous spouse) may make you insufferable on the page. For this genre, try vulnerability and relatability. Make the reader worry you might not be okay. Start with a scene or prologue where you're about to jump off a cliff. Think of Peter Alson's *Confessions of an Ivy League Bookie* and comedian Sarah Silverman's *The Bedwetter*. The subcategory Sick-Lit includes Elizabeth Wurtzel's *Prozac Nation: Young and Depressed in America*, Porochista Khakpour's *Sick*, David Sheff's *Beautiful Boy: A Father's Journey through His Son's Addiction* and Esme Weijun Wang's *The Collected Schizophrenia*. As my therapist advised: "Lead the least secretive life you can." That explains why so many students

published books from my first assignment: write about your most humiliating secret. The metaphor I use for this genre is: don't sit down to write in a three-piece suit; come naked.

15. **Be Bold, Not Boring:** Just because something happened in real life is never enough reason to write it. Use fictional and poetic techniques so your nonfiction book can be a page-turner. Show full, fleshed-out scenes filled with action; don't "tell" or sum up too much. Cut out the stage directions, self-serving tangents and unending details important only to you and your mother, like your straight A report cards throughout school. I advise my students, "Don't tell the co-op board about your two abortions," meaning don't give information that isn't relevant to your plot line at hand. Focus on your topic, slow down and make it sing. Writing can always be made better with editing and "killing your darlings." That expression, attributed to William Faulkner, refers to cutting your favorite lines and stories that show how clever you are, but don't offer deeper illumination. The worst criticism my former poetry teacher, the late Joseph Brodsky, used to share was "There's no blood here," implying it's all on the surface. But you should also be artfully honest. As Emily Dickinson said, "tell it slant."

    To apply this idea to memoirs, remember that a writer doesn't have to present every single thing that happened head-on, in chronological order. You can leave out whole decades if you want. Nonfiction means it has to be true and you can't lie and shouldn't invent people who don't exist or crimes that didn't happen. Yet you can exaggerate or change minor details as long as you fess up in your author's note, which can reflect your tone. You can always use fears, fantasies, reveries, secrets, therapy sessions, journals, research and quotes to enliven and enhance the day-to-day minutiae. Just make it clear which parts are facts versus feelings, as in the line: "My dreams replayed our final date, but this time it was funny . . . "

16. **Give It Distance:** Pain and regret are great subjects to mine for memoirs. Journaling in your notebook is a soulful way to work

through trauma. Yet it's usually best to avoid publishing nonfiction when a conflict's still unresolved. If you haven't quit a substance, it's probably not the time to sell an addiction memoir. If you and your spouse are in the middle of splitting up, your book on divorce may offer too raw a perspective. I tried to publish many bad breakup and addiction memoirs that didn't work—until I was happily married, clean, sober and had come out the other end of the struggle. Despite Cat Marnell's conflicts about whether to get clean, her memoir focused on the rehab she'd gone through to get off drugs. Kerry Cohen waited until she was in her thirties to publish *Loose Girl: A Memoir of Promiscuity* about her tumultuous teenage years. While my colleague Amy Klein wrote powerful short *New York Times* pieces on her miscarriages and fertility obstacles, she didn't sell her infertility book *The Trying Game* until after she gave birth to her daughter. You might be at your hottest when you're going through a scandal, but you're not your wisest. Once it's out there with your name on it, you can't take it back if you change your mind.

You can always finish your ordeal and your pages first, then decide about publishing later.

Don't worry that your story won't be important enough or overthink all the issues your book might cause people you know. As Anne Lamott said, "You own everything that happened to you . . . If people wanted you to write warmly about them, they should have behaved better." To fight off any psychological blocks, pretend you're writing it for yourself or penning a letter to your best friend. Don't hold back, let it pour out in whatever messy form it takes. After you complete a first draft of your book or proposal, you can debate whether your topic is too controversial, or will get you in trouble with the law, employers or relatives. If so, you can revise, disguise your characters, fictionalize for a different genre or use a pseudonym. I'm close with my conservative Michigan family, but they detest my revealing memoirs, which led me to the rule I tell my classes: the first thing you write that your family hates means you found your voice.

ADVICE FROM A MEMOIR EXPERT

My colleague Betsy Lerner is a perfect memoir maven because she has seen the genre from three sides: she was a book editor for fifteen years at Houghton Mifflin and Doubleday before she became an agent with Dunow, Carlson and Lerner Literary Agency. She's worked with National Book Award–winner Patti Smith, animal scientist Temple Grandin, civil rights activist Kenji Yoshino and the late acclaimed bestsellers Lucy Greeley and Elizabeth Wurtzel. To make Lerner a triple threat, she's also published a trio of engaging first-person bestsellers of her own: *The Bridge Ladies* (2016), *Food and Loathing: A Life Measured Out in Calories* (2003) and *Forest for the Trees: An Editor's Advice to Writers* (2000), which I recommend to my students all the time. Here's her take on how to be a published memoirist.

1. **Be a Patient Packrat:** For unknown authors, the writing in a memoir has to be as great as the story and it takes time. Most of Lerner's clients spent at least five years on their memoirs, some with several previous books that didn't sell tucked away in their drawers or computer files. If you've been keeping diaries or writing blog posts, that's the best way to develop your voice, which—in memoir—is everything. (I've also found keeping scrapbooks, journals and photo albums is great for research and fact-checking.)

2. **Find an Unusual Twist:** If you're not famous with a built-in audience, you need to come up with an original story or angle that people haven't heard before. *Autobiography of a Face* (2004) chronicles how the author Lucie Grealy's face was disfigured when a third of her jawbone was removed to try to stop the spread of a rare cancer diagnosis. Temple Grandin's *The Girl Who Loved Cows, Embraced Autism and Changed the World* (2012) shows ways the author's diagnosis

actually became her superpower. In *Bettyville,* John Hodgeman leaves his life in New York to take care of his sick ninety-year-old mother in Missouri and comes to terms with his sexuality. *Bridge Ladies* depicts Lerner's mother's bridge-playing Jewish cohorts in Connecticut, the kind of group that's usually invisible.

3. **Don't Write Instead of Therapy:** Good memoirs share deeply personal conflicts. But the resultant exposure is more apt to exacerbate than solve problems. When she began *Food and Loathing,* Lerner had a fantasy that putting all the details of her eating disorder out there would somehow fix it. It didn't. Going public can actually be triggering since, when promoting a memoir, detailed questions can feel invasive and exposing—even though you wrote the book! You may want to completely resolve an issue before going public with it, or at least create boundaries and a safety net for promotion. (My young student who published a book about a date rape and her divorce felt re-traumatized when interviewers harped on those difficult subjects years after she'd finished the book. For this reason I was glad I was still in addiction recovery when I published *Lighting Up.* In fact, when sharing book news my therapist interjected, "Be careful. Press is your new cocaine!")

4. **Build Up, Don't Cut Down:** Nobody wants an angry victimized screed that's just a litany of bad things mean people did to you. Trashing others in print is too easy, especially for a memoirist who has all the power. Many early drafts of memoirs criticize the author's exes, bosses, bullies, families, religion, suburban upbringing and relatives. In *Bridge Ladies,* Lerner dignified and gave voice to the passing breed of older Jewish women in the suburbs like her mother. *Them, Glass Castle* and *Memory Palace* are examples of books that searched to understand, not undermine, difficult relatives.

5. **Are You Playing the Shocking Sweepstakes?** As editor of *Prozac Nation* (1994), Lerner suggested her then twenty-seven-year-old author tone down some passages about sex and drugs. Wurtzel

actually amped it up, with more exhibitionistic memoirs like *Bitch* (1998), *The Bitch Rules* (2000) and *More Now Again, a Memoir of Addiction* (2001). She later published provocative, controversial pieces about finding her real father, the breakup of her marriage and the breast cancer that tragically killed her at age fifty-two. ("I am a con artist and cancer is my final con," she wrote.) Yet she didn't necessarily benefit from the notoriety that came from her disclosures. Yes, she got lots of attention, especially when she posed naked on the cover of *Bitch*, but it wasn't the attention she wanted. (One of her last exchanges, a friend tweeted, quoted William S. Burrough's *Naked Lunch:* "Hustlers of the world, there is one mark you cannot beat: the mark inside.") Ask yourself: Why are you writing this? Are you trying to make money or get attention from shock value? Will it help you or others in the long run? Is this what you want to be known for forever?

6. **Reconsider Selling Something You May Regret:** Lerner once ignited controversy at a panel I moderated when she admitted she had regrets about publishing *Food and Loathing* because, at the end of the day, it wasn't cathartic. On the contrary, she regretted her decision to spill her guts. As an agent and editor, she's seen the same results for many writers. Timing is important. Write what you need to write, but you have to be ready to publish it. While memoirists have explored such topics as heroin addiction, incest, anal sex and orgies, just because you can sell a book doesn't mean you should. Before going public with your biggest secrets, try to wait and get a little distance from it and first discuss it with a mentor, doctor, spouse or therapist.

7. **There Are Many Ways to Get Out There:** Not everybody can get published in the *New York Times*. But Lerner once found an author from their Ted Talk. And Lerner's then sixteen-year-old daughter discovered *The Friend Zone* author Abby Jiminez on YouTube. Lerner gave her intrepid teenager a third of the commission which paid way better than babysitting. My former student

Zack McDermott launched his beautiful mental health memoir *Gorilla and the Bird* with a piece on *Gawker*. Many other authors were discovered on radio, TV, podcasts, Twitter, Instagram Stories, Facebook Live, TikTok and YouTube. Finding a medium to showcase your talent might help an agent find you.

CHAPTER 2

Biographies

HOW TO BOTCH BIOGRAPHY

1. **Pick a Subject Done to Death:** No matter that there are thousands of books already published about Shakespeare. That just means he's popular enough for another.

2. **Choose Someone Completely Obscure:** Your grandmother's cousin was a really nice lady. Surely there's an audience interested in the story of an average woman who lived a modest life.

3. **Settle Scores:** Use this project as an excuse to malign the reputation of your ex-boss or former spouse forever.

4. **Chronicle Your Own Connection:** Use first person to tell personal stories about you and your subject throughout, forgetting that's called a memoir.

5. **Pitch a Personal Icon You Can't Criticize:** Just quote people who knew and adored your subject, ignoring that hagiographies are considered more ballyhoo than book.

6. **Stay Superficial:** Why waste months doing your own research when there's *People* magazine and Wikipedia?

7. **Plagiarize:** Cut and paste from all the other accounts, with no attributions. The material is old, so nobody will notice.

8. **Stay Home:** Google is so great, there's no need to visit a library or actually meet anyone in person who knew your subject.

9. **Write the Whole Book First:** Since your father loved Joe DiMaggio, just write 300 pages about him, even though all biographies are sold from proposals, not full manuscripts.

10. **Give It Six Months:** Assume you'll finish your bio in less than a year, unlike those slowpokes who put in a decade and won Pulitzer Prizes and National Book Awards.

BETTER BETS FOR BIOGRAPHERS

Unlike first-person autobiography and memoir accounts of your own life, a biography is the story of another person's life written by someone else. In the Western World, it traces back to 5th century BCE with the poet Ion of Chios's brief sketches of his famous contemporaries Pericles and Sophocles, notes Encyclopedia Britannica. In the 9th century, *The Life of Charlemagne* (also known as King Charles the Great), by a dedicated servant of his named Einhard, was close to a full modern biographical book. It had extensive info on Charlemagne's background and character, physical descriptions, political and historical annals of the day, and a firsthand account of his reign. Though it took until the 17th century for books like this to be called biographies.

The world's best early biography, the Encyclopedia maintains, is Scots lawyer James Boswell's *Life of Samuel Johnson LL.D* (1791). It set forth principles for biographical composition that still stand: the writer must tell the truth to recreate a real person, research, use interviews and eyewitness accounts. Someone doesn't have to be famous to be a worthy subject. Yet most are.

Americans aped the English, following the claim by Thomas Carlyle that "the history of the world is but the biography of great men," in *On Heroes, Hero-Worship and the Heroic in History*. The most common subjects have been US presidents. Wikipedia notes that the first book on George Washington, by Mason Locke Weems in 1800, added the mythology about Washington admitting to his father he couldn't lie about cutting down a cherry tree in a later edition and became an instant bestseller, setting the revealing tone for books to come. By the mid-19th century, a distinction appeared between mass biography and literary opus, reflecting the difference between high culture and middle class that still exists. Thanks to an expanding reading public, affordable paperback editions of biographies became popular and remain so.

These days you can find sequences of short biographies by well-known authors—covering mostly famous men—commissioned by the Penguin Lives and Applewood Books, along with children's versions from Grosset and Dunlap and Random House's "Who Was" series (which all offer books on Abe Lincoln). To update that, in 2020 Plume publishers presented a wildly engaging four-part current Queens of Resistance quartet "saluting beloved boss ladies in Congress" about Nancy Pelosi, Maxine Waters, Alexandria Ocasio-Cortez and Elizabeth Warren, by Krishan Trotman and Brenda Jones, which ran about 200 pages each.

More often, biographical tomes are door stoppers. The longest is the serial of Sir Winston Churchill, started by his son Randolph in 1968 and continued by Martin Gilbert with eight sequels and sixteen companion volumes filling 10 million words. Robert Caro's lauded quartet launched with *The Years of Lyndon Johnson: The Path to Power* (1982) is 1,405 pages, making Julia Bard's 752-page *Victoria: The Queen* (2016) seem short and breezy. They can be big-ticket hardcovers; top biographies receive million-dollar advances, though comparably.com says US biographers make on average $68,000 a year. If you're good at research and reporting, it's an excellent debut genre for an aspiring author because you're riding in on a well-known person's coattails. If you choose someone famous or popular, you immediately appropriate their fan base—especially if you're offering to reveal secret and long-buried facts their fans don't already know.

Biographies usually divide into two categories: authorized and unauthorized. Authorized means the subject—or their heirs—have either picked or sanctioned the choice of author. That can sometimes be problematic and lead to accusations of hagiography, as when Philip Roth shared all of his papers with Blake Bailey before he died for the fascinating (albeit scandal-prone) 2021 *Philip Roth: The Biography.*

Even if someone doesn't want to be the subject of your book, you can legally publish one that's unauthorized. To avoid lawsuits, you may have to prove it's accurate and that you haven't committed libel, invaded privacy, misappropriated, infringed on copyright or breached confidence. Unfortunately, the misuse of First Amendment rights perpetuated a cottage industry of "kiss and tell" bios that pillage the dead. Albert Goldman's *The Lives of John Lennon* (1988) accuses the late Beatle of being an anti-Semitic, dyslexic, bisexual, schizophrenic drug user. Joyce Carol Oates called this kind of a book "pathography" in a *New York Times* piece, maintaining that it centers on "dysfunction and disaster, illness and pratfalls, failed marriages and failed careers, alcoholism and breakdowns and outrageous conduct."

In the early Christian church, hagiographies were studies of saints and ecclesiastical leaders. In current day, calling a book a "hagiography" is an insult implying a subject is so exalted, the book is "puffery" or "PR." On the other extreme, unauthorized "pathographers," who make big bucks taking down an icon, are worse: the print equivalent of paparazzi. J. Randy Taraborrelli—author of sensationalistic bios on the Kennedys, Madonna, Elizabeth Taylor and Diana Ross—was sued for $100 million by Motown founder Berry Gordy for libel and invasion of privacy in *Michael Jackson: The Magic and the Madness* (1991). In an out-of-court settlement, the author had to delete passages from the book that libeled Gordy.

Kitty Kelly, who has trashed Oprah, the Bushes, the British royal family and Jaqueline Kennedy Onassis, allegedly earned a $3.5 million advance to skewer Nancy Reagan. But some of her fees go to lawyers defending her against lawsuits for libel, maliciousness, misappropriation, plagiarism and to halt publication of her book (which Frank Sinatra tried). Kelly claims to have never lost a case, but the court of public opinion has deemed her "a professional sensationalist," "consummate gossip monger," and a "poison pen" who writes "Kitty litter."

While it would be rare to lose a lawsuit and be imprisoned over accidental mistakes in a biography, in one infamous case, author Clifford Irving published a book allegedly written "as told to" Irving by billionaire recluse Howard Hughes. Hughes sued, Irving admitted he'd made it up and went to jail for seventeen months. When he got out, he published *The Hoax* (1981), which led to a biopic starring Richard Gere as Irving. (Note: plagiarizing and prison aren't my recommendations for a stunt memoir, novel or biography.)

Lawsuits against writers, which publishers don't cover, are so common in this field that biographers often get Errors and Omissions (E and O) insurance. (I know someone who paid $3,000 of his own dime for it.) Similar to malpractice insurance for doctors, this is a professional liability policy against libel and defamation that covers judgments, settlements and defense costs for authors. There's also media liability insurance offered by the Authors Guild since writing about real people—alive and dead—carries special risks that can result in costly damages and legal fees.

As an author who researched acclaimed biographer Laurence Bergreen, I prefer fair-minded literary works that illuminate their subject. I encourage someone aspiring to break into this genre to pick someone they respect who is worthy of years and pages. A favorite I often recommend is the 608-page *Malcolm X: A Life of Reinvention* (2011) by Columbia professor Manning Marable, who spent two decades on the definitive scholarly work of a complex man he admired. The book turned out to be Marable's life's opus. He died right before it won the 2012 Pulitzer Prize for history.

My least favorite is a critical reflection of my late cousin, the bestselling novelist Howard Fast, an early mentor. The biographer pretended to be a fan of Fast's, emailing "I would like to hear from all those who loved Howard, respected him (rightly so), and have stories to tell." I shared amusing memories showing Howard's generosity and support. It turned out the biographer vehemently opposed my relative's leftwing politics as a one-time member of the Communist party. In his book, he moralistically took Fast to task for his fame, past love affairs, and earning millions of dollars writing more than one hundred books that made it to the big and small screen, including *Spartacus*. He misappropriated details from pages I'd written about my cousin as a harmlessly flirtatious eighty-two-year-old widower at my wedding, inaccurately implying Fast was a sexual predator. These are the kind of morally questionable techniques that led Janet Malcolm to proclaim, "Every journalist is a murderer." Perhaps the biographer's motive was jealousy, since he never published a novel and only sold a few biographies to university presses, known for paying low or no advances.

Aside from these kind of takedown trash-fests, authorized and unauthorized books, there's another kind of bio I call "the connection to fame book," where an author chronicles the life of someone they met and admire, out of respect or love. My colleague Gabrielle Selz launched *Light on Fire: The Art and Life of Sam Francis* (2021) after meeting Francis as a kid and admiring his abstract paintings. Kavita Das, a former student, was introduced to the Indian singer Lakshmi Shankar when she stayed with Das's family in New York. She became Das's favorite artist, on and off stage, inspiring *Poignant Song: The Life and Music of Lakshmi Shankar* (2019). These are third-person studies, though sometimes in an intro or foreword, the author discloses their initial connection to their subject.

Be aware that biography is a different form than a first-person exploration like Sigrid Nunez's *Sempre Susan: A Memoir of Susan Sontag* (2014), recounting Sontag's influence on her work and life, or *Here We Are: My Friendship with Philip Roth* (2020) by Benjamin Taylor. While Mary L. Trump's *Too Much and Never Enough: How My Family Created the World's Most Dangerous Man* is promoted as a "revelatory, authoritative portrait of Donald J. Trump," it's a personal memoir. Biographies are third person and require research, facts, quotes and insights from many people other than yourself.

HOW TO LAUNCH A BIOGRAPHY

1. **Start Small:** Try publishing a short profile of your subject. David Margolick's riveting *New York Times* article about a multi-million-dollar family lawsuit helped sell *Undue Influence: The Epic Battle for the Johnson and Johnson Fortune* (1993). Julia Flynn Siler's *Wall Street Journal* piece on the Mondavi family led to her *New York Times* bestseller *The House of Monday: The Rise and Fall of An American Wine Dynasty* (2007).

2. **Push Your Platform:** There's a reason Korean-American political science professor Chong-Sik Lee published biographies of Korean leaders while Cuban-American professor Alfred J. Lopez tackled two books about José Martí, a polarizing Cuban revolutionary. As a legal reporter, David Margolick was ideal to chronicle a major lawsuit. A social justice journalist from a family steeped in Indian culture, Das was perfect for *Poignant Song* (2018). Sheila Weller is from the same Hollywood neighborhood as Carrie Fisher, and the romantic triangle that ruined her mother and father's marriage mirrored the split of her subjects' parents' Debbie Reynolds and Eddie Fisher in *Carrie Fisher: A Life on the Edge* (2019). Selz grew up in the art world, the setting of *Light on Fire: The Art and Life of Sam Francis* (2021).

3. **Uncover Secrets:** Researching 18th century France, Tom Reiss found that General Alex Dumas, the father of novelist Alexandra Dumas, hid an incredible secret: he was the son of a Black slave. Reiss resurrected him in his Pulitzer Prize–winning *The Black Count: Revolution, Betrayal and the Real Count of Monte Crisco* (2012). Selz learned that the art historical information about Sam Francis was based on a fundamental lie and the truth was even more incredible. While reading through archives for another project, Judy Batalion—the granddaughter of Polish Holocaust survivors—stumbled on stories in Yiddish that led to *The Light of Days: The Untold Story of Women Resistance Fighters in Hitler's Ghetto* (2021), now a bestseller optioned for a movie by Steven Spielberg.

4. **Research Means More Than Google:** When Laurence Bergreen wanted to learn more about songwriter Irving Berlin, he went to many libraries to scan through microfilm of old newspaper articles too old to be online. In one he found a story on the first time Irving Berlin sang at a club when he was a fourteen-year-old singing waiter and even the lyrics to that first song. He did in-depth interviews with more than one hundred people, liberally using the transcription of those tapes throughout his book.

5. **Rediscover Someone:** There have been about 4,500 US books published about Donald Trump from 2016 to fall of 2021, according to *The Guardian.* Instead of making the obvious choice of a famous politician, find a worthy person who was never the subject of a full-length study before. Blake Bailey's *Tragic Honesty: The Life and Work of Richard Yates* (2004) was the first in-depth look at the late novelist whom Bailey revered. In *Flash: The Making of Weegee the Famous* (2018), Christopher Bonanos offered the only comprehensive biography of the infamous newspaperman, photographer and huckster. Sonia Purnell's *A Woman of No Importance: The Untold Story of the American Spy Who Helped Win World War II* (2019) uncovered the story of Virginia Hall, a shockingly overlooked heroine.

6. **Read Biographies, History *and* Fiction:** Bergreen was enthralled with Richard Ellman's James Joyce biography and Edmund Morris's trilogy about Teddy Roosevelt. Selz's mother was interviewed by Patricia Boswell about their neighbor Diane Arbus and, as a teenager, gave Selz a copy of her book which fascinated her. While you want your biography to be factual and filled with new material, studying recent award-winning novels set in a similar time frame could show you how to employ great narrative structure, color and drama to make your story more exciting.

7. **Find Your Community:** There are many groups you should check out, including The Biographers Club (based in London), The Biography Society (in France), The Center for Biographical

Research, Center for the Study of Transformative Lives (at New York University), Biographers Guild of New York, The Washington Biography Group, Personal Historian Facebook Group and Biographers International Organization, which has an annual conference you can attend.

8. **Add a Modern Spin:** Pitching a short piece to a newspaper or magazine editor, I remind my students to answer: Why me? Why you? Why now? That's also true of biographies, where you can make your subject more relevant by providing a new or newsworthy prism. Rebecca Skloot's *The Immoral Life of Henrietta Lacks* (2010), chronicling how a Black patient and her family were kept from knowing about the medical world's use of her cancerous cells, and Margo Lee Shetterly's *Hidden Figures: The American Dram and the Untold Story of the Black Women Who Helped Win the Space Race* (2016) plays up a contemporary social justice angle. Offering an important revisionist history of overlooked Black female citizens was a way to make both projects more relevant to current audiences.

9. **Don't Stop at Top US Publishers:** As you can guess, the biggest houses pay the largest advances and have the most PR. Yet if they reject your proposal, you still have many options. Often small, indie, foreign and academic presses pay less (or no) money up front, but sometimes offer more chances for prestige, awards, reviews and royalties from the back end (since critics would be more apt to review a book from Harvard University Press than Harlequin, now a division of HarperCollins). When Selz was told "art stories have small audiences," she persisted and sold her book about Sam Francis to the University of California Press. After US publishers weren't sure an Indian singer would have an American readership, Kavita Das sold *Poignant Song: The Life and Music of Lakshmi Shankar* to HarperCollins India (2019), which made it widely available in America anyway.

10. **Have Company:** Group biographies illuminate a theme or cluster of people behind a movement, like *Band of Brothers*, Stephen

E. Ambrose's 1992 study of a parachute infantry company during World War II (which led to a mini-series) and Sherill Tippins' *The February House: The Story of Auden, Carson McCullers, Jane and Paul Bowles, Benjamin Britten and Gypsy Rose Lee, Under One Roof in Wartime America* (2005). I loved Sheila Weller's bestseller *Girls Like Us: Carole King, Joni Mitchell, Carly Simon—and the Journey of a Generation* (2008) and her follow-up *The New Sorority: Diane Sawyer, Katie Couric, Christiane Amanpour, and the (Ongoing, Imperfect, Complicated) Triumph of Women in TV News* (2014). The aforementioned Margo Lee Shetterly's *Hidden Figures* (2016) also resulted in an Oscar-nominated movie.

11. **Try a Topic Other Than a Person:** While there's sometimes cross-over between biographies, history, culture, politics and scientific nonfiction, structuring your book about a subject as if it is a biography could be fruitful. My old friend Maggie Paley profiled a body part in *The Book of the Penis* (1999). Dr. Siddhartha Mukherjee's *A Biography of Cancer* (2010) is a masterpiece. My former student Joseph Alexiou's *Gowanus: Brooklyn's Curious Canal* (2015) tells the story of the famously foul canal from inception to current day. The *New York Times* called it "a loving and skillfully rendered portrait."

12. **No Book Is Definitive:** Writers can always bring new information and a different angle for a new book on a well-covered subject, according to Selz. There were already several books out on Caroline Frazier's subject when she wrote her 640-page *Prairie Fires: The American Dreams of Laura Ingalls Wilder* (2017). Frazier told Wilder's story within the context of American history and our national predilection for self-mythologizing and creating false narratives of self-reliance. It won the Pulitzer Prize. Though please don't pitch anything else on Donald Trump or Lyndon B. Johnson.

EXPERT ADVICE FROM A FAMED BIOGRAPHER

Instead of name-dropping him, why not go right to the biographer's mouth? Laurence Bergreen is the author of nine acclaimed and best-selling biographies including James Agee, Louis Armstrong, Marco Polo, Magellan, Columbus, Casanova and *In Search of a Kingdom: Frances Drake, Elizabeth I and the Perilous Birth of the British Empire* (2021). He offered seven pieces of advice to aspiring biographers.

1. **Follow Personal Connections:** Studying at Harvard, Bergreen became fascinated by the work of his fellow alumnus James Agee, who'd lived in the same dorm. After getting a job in television, Bergreen's boss Robert Saudek mentioned he'd been Agee's college roommate and promised to reveal wild stories of Agee. Bergreen took him up on it and his first biography—of Agee—was born. Selz and Das also chronicled people they were literally and emotionally linked to. Is there a luminary you met once that may be a good subject for a book?

2. **Steep Yourself in Research:** Bergreen spent five years researching his book on Berlin. He wanted to explore the paradoxes of the famous Russian-born Jewish composer of *White Christmas, Easter Parade* and *God Bless America* beyond his feel-good patriotic lyrics and rags-to-riches story. "Researching is the ultimate test for me. If I get more interested the more I discover about someone, that's an indication I've found my subject. If I get bored, I need to look for someone more engaging," he said. Because it can take so long, he works on a few projects simultaneously to see which pans out.

3. **Propose a Miniature Model of Your Book:** When pitching his biographies, Bergreen argued for his subject's importance and relevance, explaining why this book needs to be written now. After an editor once commented on his idea, "Oh that sounds like homework," he made sure his proposals were as exciting as the book pages they led to.

4. **Heed Professional Advice:** Agents and editors might know more about what sells in the marketplace than you do. After editing Bergreen's book on James Agee, Viking editor Joe Kanon suggested he do a book on Irving Berlin. Although writing about a famous musician had never occurred to him, Bergreen gave it a try and it turned into a big hit.

5. **Don't Be Discouraged by Similar Books on Your Subject:** While researching Agee, Bergreen heard another bio on the author was in the works. That fueled him to finish his faster. The other book never came out. Meanwhile, there were already shelves filled with Al Capone. So Bergreen focused on the surprisingly emotional side of the gangster hurt by anti-Italian prejudice, and a devoted son and father to a child who was partially deaf (because of the untreated syphilis Capone passed onto his wife, Bergreen alleged). He may have done his job too well. Ironically, people told him Capone—the poster boy for crime and violence—came off intelligent and considerate, whereas Berlin, an honest, moral genius, was found to be a "sonofabitch."

6. **Don't Stay Specialized:** You may need a "platform" or connection for a debut biography, as Bergreen had with Agee. But once you're established, you can spread out for future projects. Not wanting to be pigeonholed, Bergreen later tackled such divergent characters as Louis Armstrong, Christopher Columbus, Sir Frances Drake and Queen Elizabeth. Researching books became his excuse to travel the world, pursue varied interests and read "indiscriminately."

7. **Narrow Your Book's Focus:** A modern biography doesn't necessitate a full-scale cradle-to-grave chronicle. It can cross over to narrative nonfiction by centering on a certain time period or event. Bergreen's *Columbus* told the story of his subject's four main voyages, spanning twelve years. Magellan focused on his traveling the globe during a three-year span. *In Search of a Kingdom* covers one decade, beginning with Drake's circumnavigation (1577–1580),

which set the stage for the rivalry of Battle of the Spanish Armada (1588). You don't have to start with birth. Begin with the most dramatic part of your subject's life, then weave in a subject's childhood and past later.

CHAPTER 3

How-To Books/Self-Help

HOW *NOT* TO HOW-TO

1. **Know Nothing About Your Subject**: Pick an area where you have no real knowledge or experience, since everyone would love to hear a personal trainer pontificating about how to build a house. You're sick of your field anyway, so here's a way to explore new territory.

2. **Avoid Research:** So what if there's already many books about how to win elections by people who work in the political arena and, as a hairdresser, you have no knowledge or wisdom to add and don't even vote? No problem—their stuffy opinions are too complicated. You'll bring a freshness and originality to the topic.

3. **Forget to Contact Experts**: The big shots out there already have huge platforms, jobs and audiences, so why should you add to it by quoting them?

4. **Skip Advice:** Write 300 pages about your own bad relationship history ending with meeting your fantastic spouse. It can chronicle how you did it, so that's a good enough how-to, right?

5. **Oppose Another Hit Book:** Call yours "He *Is* Just That Into You" or "How *Not* To Win Friends and Influence People," riffing off a long-ago bestseller—instead of coming up with your own original idea.

6. **Plagiarize Other Authors:** It's already on the internet, so that means you can steal the work of other people and cobble it together to make your own book, right? I mean, like, there's not even any bylines on Wikipedia, so it's all up for grabs.

7. **Recycle Advice Everybody Already Knows:** To beat cancer, you need a good doctor to catch it early and a healthy lifestyle. Sometimes the obvious stuff bears repeating, doesn't it?

8. **Avoid Current Trends and Political Correctness:** Forget about all those plus-size models and body positivity activists and call your book *How to Lose Weight to Get Skinny and Beautiful.*

9. **Skirt Fact Checking and Updating:** Make sure to mention people who have died without indicating they have passed away, cite organizations that are no longer in business, web articles that have been taken down and websites that are defunct.

10. **Stay Hyper-Local:** Include entire pages listing the best doctors, lawyers and accountants in your town—even though you want a mainstream publisher and their books are national—or international. Isn't there like that big rule to write what you know?

SAVVIER WAYS TO SELF-HELP

Is there a particular skill, talent or hard-won wisdom that you feel compelled to publicly share? If, like me, you're a busybody know-it-all who thinks your solutions can fix the world, this may be the genre for you.

How-to books are also called "self-help," "self-improvement" or "service journalism" because they provide a service that offers advice by experts. They usually offer ways to make someone's love life, home life, finances or health better faster. The title originated in 1859 with the internationally bestselling book *Self Help* by Scottish journalist Samuel Smile, a government reformer whom the magazine referred to as "the Victorians' personal coach," noted *The Economist.* Dale Carnegie, a pioneer of the modern self-improvement genre, was a traveling salesman who taught a class in public speaking that became his book *How to*

Win Friends and Influence People (1936). It sold more than 30 million copies, making it one of the bestselling books of all time, according to Goodreads.

To familiarize yourself with more recent specimens of this lucrative genre, think of all the self-help gurus who became bestselling authors by writing books in their area of expertise: Suzy Orman (finances), Martha Stewart (domesticity), Dr. Drew Pinsky (addiction), Dr. Sanjay Gupta (medicine), Dr. Ruth Westheimer (sex), Deepak Chopra (spirituality), Iyana Vanzant (relationship coaching), Tim Ferris (career), Judge Judy Sheindlin (legalese), Jonathan and Drew Scott (home renovation) and Marie Kondo (organizing consultant). Though Kondo lost me when she showed off that she only keeps thirty books while continuing to publish what literary snobs I admire refer to as "ooks."

You don't have to be rich and famous with your own TV show, or have a PhD to publish a self-help book. Indeed, my "platforms" have been having an obsession (and some success) with amateur matchmaking, the subject of *Secrets of a Fix-Up Fanatic: How to Meet and Marry Your Match* (Random House, 2005). Chronicling how I set up thirty marriages, it's filled with advice on how to meet your soulmate. Being a recovering addict was the background I employed while coauthoring my *Unhooked: How to Quit Anything* (Skyhorse Publishing, 2012) with Dr. Frederick Woolverton, my addiction specialist who'd spent thirty years helping patients battle substance abuse. I used my years of publishing and teaching writing as a platform for two how-to books on writing: *Only as Good as Your Word: Writing Lessons From My Favorite Literary Gurus* (Seal Press, 2007) and *The Byline Bible: Get Published in Five Weeks* (Writer's Digest Books, 2018). While they are sometimes listed under the subcategories of "business" or "writing books," I see them as "how to" since they offer advice on how to improve your work—and outlook.

For this kind of book—more than others—you definitely need a "platform." In publishing that basically refers to having experience or an expertise, a metaphoric or literal stage or megaphone that can help you reach a wide audience. It can take the form of a university where you're a longtime known professor in your arena, a hospital or company where you work, a TV, radio show or podcast with many fans, or a vast social media following. Even if you're young or inexperienced, you may have hidden knowledge it would be beneficial to share.

HOW TO START YOUR HOW-TO

1. **Determine Your Greatest Gifts:** Figure out what you are best at. If you were going to teach a class, what would it be? What's your job or award-winning subject? What was your major at school? What's your favorite hobby, ability or power others don't possess?
2. **Examine What Works Well in Your Life:** If you don't have a graduate degree or decades of mastery in a sport or an art, think about your family unit. Are you happily married for decades, for example, or a parent, or have three beloved pets?
3. **What Obstacles Have You Overcome?** Did you come out as gay, bisexual or trans in a way that might help others? Do you, your parents, spouse or children have a disability you've struggled with? Did you pull yourself out of poverty and debt?
4. **Up Your Platform:** If you fear you don't have enough of an audience or expertise, you can vastly increase it by publishing a timely provocative short op-ed or essay (subject of my book *Byline Bible*) which can lead to podcast, radio and TV appearances. My student Caroline Koster's first piece in the *Wall Street Journal,* "Politics Won't Come Between My Appalachian Cousins and Me," landed her on FOX and Sarah Herrington was interviewed on Canada's NPR after her *New York Times* op-ed "Yoga Teachers Need a Code of Ethics." If you're having trouble finding paid freelance work, consider writing a free advice column or sharing your knowledge on your blog or one with a set readership, like Medium or *Psychology Today.*
5. **Embrace Social Media:** Some young students trash Facebook and Twitter, saying they're for old people, forgetting that "old people"

still run most of publishing. Lots of books launched directly through social media posts and it's free. On advice from an agent, this technophobe learned to increase my followers on Facebook, Twitter, Instagram and LinkedIn so I can now reach a million people with a message or link in less than one minute, perhaps why I was able to sell three recent book projects.

6. **What Do You Have That People Want?** After being fixed up with my great husband and setting up several couples that got married, I noticed many single acquaintances were coming to me to ask advice. When I quit smoking and drinking, lots of friends asked me how I did it. And as I published more work, students wanted to know how they could too. These seeds eventually led to my how-to's.

7. **Get a Great Title/Subtitle With a Goal:** The best monikers for how-to books make it clear what they are promising, like Dale Carnegie's aforementioned *How to Win Friends and Influence People* and Jen Sincero's 2013 bestseller *You Are a Badass: How to Stop Doubting Your Greatness and Start Living an Awesome Life.* I tried to do this in my own titles *Secrets of a Fix-Up Fanatic: How to Meet and Marry Your Match, Unhooked: How to Quit Anything* and *The Byline Bible: Get Published in Five Weeks.*

8. **Use Numbers or a Time Frame:** Since people want a simple, practical structure to improve their lives, many self-help books offer numerical breakdowns: Don Miguel Ruiz's *The Four Agreements: A Practical Guide to Personal Freedom* (Amber-Allen Publishing, 1997), Shonda Rhimes's *Year of Yes: How to Dance It Out, Stand in the Sun and Be Your Own Person* (Simon and Schuster, 2015) and Stephen R. Covey's *The 7 Habits of Highly Effective People: Powerful Lessons in Personal Change* (Simon and Schuster, 1989).

9. **Map Out a Chronological Strategy:** Figuring out the plans of action for my how-to books to make my ideas concrete, I wrote a list of steps to achieve the transformation goal, from start to finish. Ibram X. Kendi's award-winning book *How to Be An Anti-Racist,* a hybrid memoir with a how-to manifesto (Random House, 2019),

starts with definitions of what a racist and an anti-racist is. Robert Greene's bestseller *The 48 Laws of Power* (Penguin, 1998) begins with an expanded table of contents listing the forty-eight laws, with several sentences beneath each one.

10. **Write Like a Best Friend or Favorite Teacher**: While you're the expert sharing your experience and knowledge, don't come off like a show-off who feels superior to your readers. Be clear, funny, humble and self-deprecating. On an Amazon review of *Byline Bible,* someone I didn't know wrote that I'd accomplished "what Lionel Trilling said about George Orwell: 'He communicates to us the sense that what he has done, any one of us could do.'" For a teacher and self-help writer, that's the ultimate praise.

11. **Try a First-Person Preface:** Even if you're using a third-person narrative, I like knowing at the start the author's motivation for writing the book. In *Positive Illusions: Creating Self-Deception and the Healthy Mind* (Basic Books, 1989), Dr. Shelley E. Taylor tells us how, as a college student, she worked at a mental institution and first noticed the mindset in trauma patients that inspired her theories. While *Unhooked* shares case studies of addiction patients, my coauthor Frederick Woolverton admits in the first paragraph, "Treating addicts has never been just about work, scientific data, or abstract theories for me. I am particularly sensitive to both the literal and the hidden repercussions of addiction because as a child I was severely traumatized by an alcoholic parent."

12. **Quote Other Experts:** I enjoy hearing first-person stories and advice from smart authors who have overcome trauma or difficulties in life. Yet I don't know anybody who struggles through obstacles and comes out the other end who hasn't had help, whether it's from parents, professors, doctors, shrinks, books or predecessors in their field. While you don't want to dilute your own voice by inundating the reader with other people's adages, it makes you look generous to quote—and correctly attribute—the wisdom that helped you.

SELF-HELP SUCCESSES

Here are some great how-to books that people from my classes and writing workshops have published about their proficiencies and obsessions over the years.

The Trying Game: Get Through Fertility Treatment and Get Pregnant Without Losing Your Mind (Ballantine, 2020), about Amy Klein's infertility battle before having her daughter, helps women who are having trouble having a child. It's based on her *New York Times* Motherlode columns on the subject.

In *The Pleasure Plan: One Woman's Search for Sexual Healing* (HCI Inc., 2020), author Laura Zam shows how, as a survivor of sexual abuse, she learned to enjoy sex again.

Amy B. Scher's *How to Heal Yourself from Anxiety When No One Else Can* (Llewellyn Publications, 2019) and *How to Heal Yourself When No One Else Can: A Total Self-Healing Approach for Mind, Body and Spirit* (Llewellyn Publications, 2016), both chronicle how the author took her health into her own hands when she almost died from Lyme disease. She shares the coping techniques she uses as a mind-body coach.

In *Get to the Point: Sharpen Your Message and Make Your Words Matter* (Berrett-Koehler Publishers, 2017), Joel Schwartzberg, a public speaker and communications executive, teaches how anyone could improve their verbal skills.

In *Never Try to Drink a Chinese Woman Under the Table: Plus Other Fun and Practical Tips for Doing Business in China and at Home* (Strategic Media Books, 2014), the authors Jim Fox and Richard Bradspies offer tips they learned doing international business in Asia.

In *You're Accepted: Getting into the Right College by Getting to Know Your True Self* and *Earn It: A Stress-Free and Proven Approach to Getting into Top MBA Programs* (Hay House, 2013), Katie Malachuk, who has degrees from Harvard and Stanford and also taught yoga, shares her wisdom with aspiring students.

In *Confessions of a Casting Director: Help Actors Land Any Role With Secrets from Inside the Audition Room* (HarperCollins, 2013), longtime award-winning casting director Jen Rudin spills insider tips for actors looking to land roles in theatre, TV and film.

Happily married psychologist Dr. Diana Kirschner's appearances on radio and TV led to her relationship book *Love in 90 Days: The Essential Guide to Finding Your Own True Love* (Hachette, 2009). It did so well she penned the sequel *Sealing the Deal: The Love Mentor's Guide to Lasting Love* (Hachette, 2010).

Bruce Frankel's *What Should I Do With the Rest of My Life: True Stories of Finding Success, Passion, and New Meaning in the Second Half of Life* (Avery, 2010) starts with the author going back to graduate school at age thirty-two.

Sherry Amatenstein's *The Complete Marriage Counselor: Relationship Advice from America's Top 50 Couples Therapists* (Adams Media, 2010) shares advice from the LMSW's couples counseling sessions, while also quoting top relationship experts.

In *One Person/Multiple Careers: A New Model for Work/Life Success* (Hachette, 2007), Marci Alboher, an author/speaker/coach who wrote the Career column for the *New York Times*, discloses her theories why "slashing" through multifaceted professional lives is the wave of the future.

My former student Lauren Levin's *Same Sex in the City: So Your Prince Charming Is Really a Cinderella*, written with Lauren Blitzer (Simon and Schuster, 2006), is a guide to everything lesbian, from coming out to bisexuality to how to meet women, as well as an atlas to educate well-meaning straight people.

Sugar Shock: How Sweet and Simple Carbs Can Derail Your Life— And How You Can Get Back on Track (Berkley, 2006), by former sugar addict and coach Connie Bennett and cardiologist Dr. Stephan Sinatra, offers twenty simple, sugar-free strategies. It led to the follow-up *Beyond Sugar Shock: The 6-Week Plan to Break Free of Your Sugar Addition and Get Slimmer, Sexier and Sweeter* (Hay House, 2012).

In Susan Jane Gilman's humorous *Kiss My Tiara: How to Rule the World as a SmartMouth Goddess* (Grand Central Publishing, 2001), an outspoken feminist offers advice to women on how to stand up for what you believe in.

AN EXPERT OFFERING HELP FOR SELF-HELP

My friend Karen Salmansohn, a bestselling how-to guru whose 50+ books have sold more than 2 million copies, specializes in "self-help books for people who wouldn't be caught dead reading self-help." A former award-winning copywriter, she learned the art and magic of a funny provocative title long before it was mainstream, in books like *How to Succeed in Business Without a Penis* (1996) and *How to Be Happy, Dammit (2001),* which led to spinoffs like *Happy Habits* (2020). Here are her secrets on how to publish how-to.

1. **Visualize Your Concept and Cover:** Once she gets the words down for a new project, Salmansohn imagines it visually. She has drawn, designed and art directed many of her own manuscripts. A decade ago she taught me a trick I use to this day: when I begin a book, I create its cover, with a title, my byline and a picture or a photograph, increasing my motivation by making my book fantasy seem more concrete. Of course, sometimes publishers insist on doing your cover their way. But even if they have different ideas, I've had great luck asking my editors to consider using a specific piece of art or photograph I love, like the sculptor John Brown's rendition of five heads on *Five Men Who Broke My Heart,* the artist Donald Sultan's "Smoke Rings" photograph on the hardcover *Lighting Up,* my husband's first typewriter gracing *Only as Good as Your Word* and the dazzling design by painter Ron Agam on my current cover.

2. **Don't Trail a Trend, Start One:** If a kind of book is already out there, do something else. Figure out the next big thing that's different than what's selling now. In fact, decades after Salmansohn fought to use words like *penis* and *dammit* in her titles, it's become commonplace, so she stopped. "If everybody is zigging," she advises, "you should zag."

3. **One Idea at a Time:** Don't throw your whole life, or everything and the kitchen sink, into your first self-help project or nobody will know what it's about. Salmansohn clearly delineates her books by their single laser-like focus. Her *Penis* book centers on women's career success in a man's world. *The Clitourist: A Guide to One of the Hottest Spots on Earth* (2002) presents a comical study of female anatomy. *Prince Harming: Break Bad Relationship Patterns for Good* (2009) is about quitting toxic romantic relationships. *Life Is Long: 50+ Ways to Help You Live a Little Bit Closer to Forever* (2018) includes only health advice for longevity. Attempting to sell a book about how to fix all that's wrong in the reader's life is probably going to be too vague and general.

4. **Be More Approachable, Less Political:** Historically some self-help gurus pushed their politics. Republican Norman Vincent Peale, author of *The Power of Positive Thinking* (1952), was a fan of President Nixon. Recent Democratic candidate Marianne Williamson, author of *Tears to Triumph: Spiritual Healing for the Modern Plagues of Anxiety and Depression* (2017), is an outspoken rival of Trump. Salmansohn has remained an international bestseller by staying neutral. She's more apt to share an inspiring quote poster (like "Don't worry if someone does not like you. Most people are struggling to like themselves") with her 110,000 Instagram followers than a meme trashing the president. When her joke complaining she didn't want her name to be associated with bad people named *Karen*—a pejorative slang term for a white, racist, entitled woman—caused her to lose fans, she went back to completely non-partisan, safer posts. (After an incendiary *Wall Street Journal* op-ed I wrote alienated readers from both sides of the spectrum, my agent—who had just submitted my new memoir to editors—asked me, "Are you trying to sell political books or run for office?" Since I wasn't trying to do either, I scaled back on controversial opinion pieces which often paid $100, while books might pay 1,000 times that.)

5. **Beef Up Your Back Story:** Showing off qualities like confidence, good looks and success can make you seem hateful on the page, because you'll come off like a robotic, privileged show-off. For self-help, you may connect more emotionally with your readers if you're vulnerable and relatable. For *Prince Harming Syndrome*, Salmansohn discusses difficult breakups from her past. *The Bounce Back Book: How to Thrive in the Face of Adversity, Setbacks and Losses* (2018) reveals how she increased her reliance after a traumatic experience. You can put this story in your book's introduction, "About the author" page on Amazon, your publisher's website and on social media.

6. **Don't Get Hung Up on the Deal:** Over three decades, Salmanshon's advances have ranged from $8,000 from small presses to six figures from the biggest publishers in the world, to many in between. You don't have only one project in you and after you prove yourself, you can move on, or sideways sometimes. When I was upset about being offered a small advance, Salmansohn shared the liberating advice: "Some books are lucrative, some are labors of love and you can have both."

7. **Err on the Side of Generosity:** Working on *Life Is Long*, Salmansohn reached out to many experts in the field, quoting them by name and plugging their books. She's helped launch many other authors (myself included) and often offers beautiful blurbs for projects by younger writers and fellow self-help gurus. As she wrote in *Good Karma in a Box* (2003): make a promise to pass on positive energy every day, which helps everybody, including yourself.

CHAPTER 4

Nonfiction Book Proposals

WHAT *NOT* TO DO WHEN SUBMITTING YOUR NONFICTION BOOK PROPOSAL

1. **Email Your Op-Ed Piece Around, Asking "Want To Buy My Book about This Topic?":** Why work on an official 50-page proposal when you've already published 500 words they can read instead?
2. **Make Your Overview Boring:** Though it's the first part agents and editors will see, they'll really understand what you're doing when they get to the sample pages. The rest is just perfunctory.
3. **Omit a Compelling Argument for Your Project:** No need to research what's already out there or why your book should exist now. Publishers will love a vague diamond in the rough.
4. **Forget Chapter Breakdowns:** Sure, agents and editors insist on this section. But it's boring and tedious. You're not sure how your book will turn out anyway, so skip it.
5. **Compare Your Project to Famous Old Books:** Since you're Irish, cite *Angela's Ashes*, disregarding advice that comp titles should be recent. In fact, though your project is nonfiction, it's set on Long Island, so link it to *The Great Gatsby* to show how literary and ambitious you are.

6. **Pick Comparable Books in Different Genres:** Hey, what's the real difference between fiction, poetry and biography? When it comes down to it, it's all words, dude. It's so corporate to get hung up on categories.

7. **Avoid Publishing Anything Shorter First:** Writing a book is a great way to start. Don't waste time getting clips in newspapers and magazines like all those other writers. This way you'll stand out.

8. **Ignore Agents Who Ask for Proposals:** You've written the entire book, so why fuss with the sales tool they want? Guidelines posted on their websites are for authors who haven't produced the dazzling masterpiece you have.

9. **Send the Whole File to Agents and Editors Unsolicited:** Hey, after spending so much time writing the damn proposal, just rush it to everyone indiscriminately, to spread the word. And have it printed and mail it out in a box too, in case they missed it.

10. **Create Your Own Multi-Media Proposal:** The format publishers request is too complicated. Illustrations, emojis and broken hyperlinks are the wave of the future, don't ya think?

WISER PLANS FOR PROPOSING

While it's usually best to write the entire manuscript of fiction and poetry, it's advisable to *propose* a nonfiction book to editors *before* you finish your project. Writing anywhere from 15 to 75 double-spaced pages about your project makes more sense than spitting out the whole thing. You wouldn't want to invest years and dollars interviewing people or traveling for a biography or how-to book that nobody buys.

A book proposal is basically a business plan for your book. Its purpose is to convince a literary agent, and then an editor and publisher, that you have a viable idea for a book-length project, as well as the talent and expertise to pull it off. You have to prove it's much more than a magazine article—and that you can deliver the pages you promise on deadline. Books are expensive to make. If you hope to be paid up front for yours, you'll have to show editors you're a good bet with an idea that will potentially sell enough copies to pay back the money they'll advance you.

For an author, the benefits of pitching your project (versus finishing it) are numerous. You can gauge the interest of agents and editors before fully committing years of your life to completion. You can get paid part of an advance to fund research or the time off you'll need to do this thing. Once you have an official deal, it can help open doors to high-level sources you can interview. It's inspiring to get agents and editors to help formulate exactly what your book will be about—as well as its title, structure and purpose. Writing a proposal is a great exercise to help you figure out your focus and level of passion for your topic. Not being able to suffer through a 30-page proposal on your subject is a sign you won't be able to kick out 300 pages. Thus a proposal is a test to determine if you've picked the right project.

Nonfiction proposals allow publishers to scrutinize who you are and how you plan to focus your narrative. It benefits them to have a say about your direction early on, so they don't commit to a project that's disappointing down the road. They can steer you away from errors, like recreating a book already out there or using discredited experts or old research.

There are many ways to craft a winning proposal and again, every happy scribe might have a different success story. Over the twenty-five years I've been an author, the rules and norms have changed constantly. They vary, depending on everything from the topic, timing, platform and prose to your background, career and level of fame. (Beyonce wants to publish her grocery list? Sign on the dotted line.)

Though not famous, in one lucky case, I sold a book when an editor contacted me right after a short clip ran in a big newspaper and went viral. Another time, I struggled to write a 125-page treatise involving extensive historical research. (That was worth the effort—it became two books.) I once sweated over a proposal for a memoir that didn't sell. Undeterred, I finished 220 pages. After more rejections, I revised and updated the proposal based on the new version of the memoir and sold that to the publisher who'd previously turned down both the proposal *and* the manuscript. In a two-book deal.

HERE'S WHEN TO PROPOSE A BOOK (VERSUS COMPLETING THE ENTIRE MANUSCRIPT)

1. **Follow the Leader:** After an agent or an editor you're in contact with specifically says they want a proposal, I would heed their instructions. You can even ask them if they have a sample proposal they'd recommend you read and emulate.

2. **Stop the Presses:** If you a have a very topical story about something currently in the news like immigration, police brutality or climate change that you think—or have been advised—can sell immediately, it's worth it to try a quick, short proposal and see what kind of response you get. Although sometimes 10 pages is enough to get a book deal, always write more if that's what's requested.

3. **Get Clipped:** If you have a hot new piece out in the *New York Times*, *The New Yorker*, *The Oprah Magazine* or in another publication that went viral, or if you were on a popular TV or radio segment, you can send that link to an agent who might jump to offer you representation. Though they will probably need a finished manuscript or proposal to officially sell your book, media can make everything go faster.

4. **Money Problems**: If your book would require you to travel to other countries to trace your family's roots and you can't afford the transportation or hotel, prepare a short proposal to see if you can get an advance to cover your costs.

5. **Track Record:** If you have a popular blog, radio show or podcast, or had a self-published book out that sold very well, you can probably sell another one based on a great short proposal. As they say, when you're hot you're hot and everyone is a starfucker.

6. **If It's Broke, Fix It:** When attempting to get agents or editors to read an entire manuscript isn't working for you, shake it up. Maybe

you'll have more luck with a shorter proposal, especially because it will force you to do an overview, marketing analysis and chapter breakdown that could lead to a winning revision.

WAYS TO PROPOSE

Most nonfiction books are bought on proposals alone these days. So you might as well familiarize yourself with the elements most agents and editorial boards ask for.

1. **Title and Subtitle**: Some people basically sell books on this alone. Think: *Go the Fuck to Sleep*, the 2011 children's blockbuster book for adults parodying a lullaby. While there is a chance your future publisher might switch the name of your book, going in with a strong title will help you capture the attention of an agent and publisher.

    My memoir about my writing gurus, originally called *Lies My Mentors Told Me,* received no offers. I was told "lies" had a negative connotation and the word *mentors* was "leaden." A Seal Press editor who liked the material renamed it the more positive: *Only as Good as Your Word: Writing Lessons from My Literary Gurus.* I'm not sure which title is apter, but the initial one never sold and the latter did. Still, most of my self-generated book titles stayed, including my debut *Five Men Who Broke My Heart,* which, my editor said, immediately made her want to read it.

2. **Intro/Overview**: This section, sometimes called "About the Book," needs anywhere between 1 and 15 pages covering what your book will be about, why it's important to publish now, and where it fits into the pantheon of texts on the topic. For my book *Lighting Up*, I argued that while addiction memoirs about quitting drinking, heroin and cocaine were hugely popular, there hadn't been any about quitting nicotine and pot, though at the time 25 percent of the population smoked cigarettes or marijuana. Remember that your intro can't be boring rambles or academic notes. It should have

forward momentum and read as engagingly as the book itself, or at least as tantalizingly as the jacket copy. I try to use a similar style as the book I'm pitching. If a proposal intro is well written, it can also serve as the introduction of the book. One editor I know recalls a case where the overview was so well done, the author sold it without having to provide any more sample material.

3. **Format**: It's important that you clarify what kind of nonfiction project this is going to be. There's a huge difference between memoir, biography, self-help, anthology and investigative journalism, including which editors might consider it. Are you the only author or is there a coauthor or other contributors? You might need to provide the word count, approximate number of illustrations or photographs and the time you'll require to write the book.

   Proposals should be double-spaced, with proper grammar, spelling and punctuation. Use full-length sentences, not shorthand style, to give the publishers a good indication of your writing ability. In many cases, the advance you will receive will be predicated on the strength of your proposal; the sharper the proposal, the higher the advance.

   You can also suggest the ultimate way you'd like to see your book published—in hardcover, trade paperback, mass market and/or as an e-book. Although a few times, my fantasy of a big important hardcover followed by the paperback a year later (a common procession) was squelched by my acquiring editor's vision of a paperback original. I once argued for a hardcover so astutely they acquiesced—only to see it sell few copies and never even make it to paper (where it probably would have sold far more because the list price is cheaper). After that I found it best to follow my publishers' leads and compromise when necessary.

4. **Chapter Breakdowns**: To let a publisher know your book's content, you should pen detailed lines on what each section will cover. Again, this shouldn't read like a rough outline of post-it notes to yourself. Use anecdotes, quotes and specifics that flesh

out the prose. Make sure every chapter has a clear purpose that builds on the last section and leads to the next. Your chapter recaps should be a fascinating and dramatic read showing the emotional arc that will make editors hungry for the completed story. While my books are typically 20 to 30 chapters with the completed outlines between 3 and 6 pages, a former student once handed in a 25-page chapter breakdown and sold her memoir to HarperCollins.

5. **Author Bio:** Who are you and why should we give you money for this project? Editors are interested in your professional and writing track record, media hits, as well as a list of the classes, lectures or seminars you've taught. But don't list the now-defunct *Itty Bitty Little Online Poetry Journal* or the forty-five other obscure publications that didn't pay you in 1974. Be careful to focus your description of yourself around your topic. You can curate your autobiography to fit your premise. To publish addiction books, I revealed my former substance abuse because it gave me a platform and authority for that material. Yet it wouldn't have helped sell my manuscript about being an amateur matchmaker or my two coauthored books about the Bosnian War. (In fact, it could have hurt my chances—especially for a children's book—since it highlighted my past as a chain-smoking, drunk pothead.)

   Be careful not to overwhelm agents and editors with your life story from birth to landmark birthday. Don't mention you worked at a bank for a dozen years if you're writing about art history. Nobody will care that you have three children and nine grandchildren unless your book is about family and parenting. Read many short bios on the last book page to see what they usually include and how concise they need to be.

6. **Sample Pages:** This is the most important part. In my experience, brilliant sample material could sell a book without some of the other elements. (I once sold a memoir on the first 80 pages to an editor I knew at Random House without anything else.) Yet an

otherwise excellent proposal without at least one full great chapter attached will probably be rejected. It's customary to use the first two chapters, on average about 25 pages, although in a few cases I added the last chapter too, to show the emotional trajectory of a surprise ending. At a panel of editors and agents I moderated, a student asked a Random House editor, "What if the first chapter of your book isn't the best?" All the panelists agreed on his answer: "Revise until it is."

7. **Audience Outreach/Marketing Plan:** Who will buy your book? What kind of connections and platform do you have to reach them? A professorship at a school where you may be able to get your book on the syllabus of your class or others? One colleague mentioned all the business travel she could combine with book lectures around the country. Identify who your readers will be. If the focus of your book is a father facing a midlife crisis, write a list of who might buy this: Male Readers. Parents. People Who Are Divorced. Baby Boomers. And don't be general, add details such as how there are 76+ million Baby Boomers, and it's the largest sector of the population and an unusually self-reflective group. Writers think of editors as word people, but they love numbers. That's because statistics and specific demographics help get the sales and marketing departments on their side.

In my proposals that sold, I mentioned the academic, professional and alumni conferences where I do events and have my books for sale, along with all the editors who previously championed my work. For my memoir *The Forgiveness Tour: How to Find the Perfect Apology,* I interviewed clergy of all backgrounds to ask about their theories on apologies and forgiving. So I indicated who my new topic might appeal to and why: Everyone interested in religion. Readers who are Jewish and feminist, like me. College and graduate students. People with addiction issues, personally or in their family. Anyone who wants forgiveness. Or just those who feel they're owed an apology.

If you don't have any ideas how to widely market your book, get to work developing some. If you have zero clue how to do this, take a class or hire a ghost editor to help you, my secret weapon for selling many proposals, including my last two.

8. **Potential Publicity/Promotion:** Have you been in the newspaper or a magazine or on TV, radio or a podcast before? Would those editors or producers help publicize your book? Do you have extensive religious, charity or alumni affiliations with newsletters or magazines that would profile you? Thousands of social media followers? Would you be willing to hire an outside publicist on your own? (I once offered to do that and wound up on television six times for my first novel *Speed Shrinking*.) And here's where selling short pieces on your topic comes in. I personally add the line "I'll continue to publish essays and op-eds on my book subject in the *New York Times, Wall Street Journal, The Los Angeles Times* and *The Washington Post.*" I know it sounds like a long shot, but don't knock it until you've tried it. I've had several students nail those major bylines. As they say, "the harder I work, the luckier I get."

9. **Competitive and Comparable Title Analysis:** Publishers rely heavily on this section where you list similar titles as your own to determine where your book will fit in the marketplace. You have to find books in the same category and format as yours that have been recently published. Preferably these "comp titles" should have been out within the last five years and sold well. Try to stay in the same genre as your book. That means don't use *Harry Potter*, especially if you're pitching adult nonfiction. Beware of all overused category killers, avoiding other monstrous bestsellers like *Eat Pray Love* or *Blink* that leave all other titles in their wake. You need something more current. On the other hand, even if it's recent, you want to pick a book that has name recognition. While it doesn't have to be a blockbuster, don't overcorrect and pick a small press book that hardly made a splash, a perfect match that did not do well in the

market that nobody has heard of. That's an invitation for editors to say, "See! Books on this topic don't sell."

The Penguin Random House website offers several ways to find comp titles: Check *New York Times, USA Today* and *Publishers Weekly* bestseller lists. Reach out to local librarians or bookstores and ask. Search online at Barnes and Noble's and Amazon's "customers who also bought this" sections. Use Goodreads' discovery tool that shows similar books. Consider joining the American Booksellers Association as a "friend of bookselling" for $200 a year.

In each case, say what your book has in common with the comparable title you list, and how it is different. Do not trash any other book, even if you didn't like it or feel yours is way better. Be positive or at least neutral, and say something like "although both books follow families in peril, the other author took a political perspective, while my project has a more personal approach." Do research. For my last proposal, I did a Google search to uncover an unusual comp: an adult immigrant memoir turned middle-grade book like the (coauthored) one I was pitching. I found a perfect comparison. And it turned out the editor who'd published it was thrilled to see my praise of her success story and bought mine—after I pointed out my coauthored story was by a younger exiled male with a much darker experience of war.

10. **Bonus Points:** In the author bio section, include the link to a brilliant piece on your theme that you've recently sold—preferably to a prestigious publication. The more noteworthy the byline, the better your chances of getting a book deal based on it. Top ten from my experience are: *The New Yorker*, the *New York Times, Washington Post, O: The Oprah Magazine, Wall Street Journal, The Atlantic, Los Angeles Times, New York Magazine, Harper's* and *Time Magazine*.

Another huge plus would be supplying advance blurbs from experts in your field who love you or your work. It may not be as hard as you think, especially if you can achieve #9. Do you have any teachers, mentors, family friends, bosses or social media connections who've praised your work in the past? After a student published a piece on walking the Pacific Crest Trail, author Cheryl Strayed and *New York Times* columnist Nicholas Kristof mentioned her piece on social media. I encouraged her to ask if she could use their words as an endorsement (colloquially known as a "blurb"). They both generously agreed. Kristof's endorsement was "A lovely tribute to the healing power of wildness," and Strayed's read: "Mercy, I love this story."

SAMPLE OVERVIEW THAT SOLD

It's not uncommon for a proposal's plot, timeline or main characters to evolve or change in the course of writing and editing a book—as well as the news cycles. But it's important for you to clearly describe your story, using specific details, and explain why your book needs to be published now.

Although space and privacy concerns don't allow me to include my entire 15,000- to 50,000-word proposals, here is the 1,600-word overview—the very beginning—of the proposal that recently sold my coauthored middle-grade memoir *World In Between* (Clarion Books, HMH 2021). My coauthor and I tried to lead with a gripping, specific question to get the reader emotionally involved in the drama from the first line. We used idiosyncratic specifics to set up the character's personal journey, before pointing out the global problem he finds himself entangled in, to underscore the timeliness and importance of the book.

How does it feel to lose your home and country, watch your best friends turn on you overnight because of your religion, and have your favorite teacher put a gun to your head?

Kenan is in fifth grade, an average Muslim boy in the Balkans. He wants to be a famous athlete and works hard to get the approval of Mr. Miran, his toughest teacher who is also the soccer coach (though they call it "fudbal"). Kenan is skinny with an embarrassing three-tooth overbite. He hates when his best friends call him "Bugs Bunny" and fears he'll never be as muscular and athletic as his annoyingly tall 17-year-old brother Eldin, his parents' favorite. He has a crush on Nina, the coolest girl in his class, and tries to impress her. Sometimes his family drives him crazy, but he loves them. His worries are small.

Then the Bosnian war comes to his doorstep and he's torn from everything he's ever known.

Kenan is far from alone. Last year 68.5 million people were displaced by violent conflicts across the globe, from Syria to Somalia to Iraq. According to the United Nations, of the 25 million refugees without a place to live, half are children. Political arguments over building a Mexican wall, ripping families apart at the border, and instituting Muslim travel bans dominate the news cycle and show no sign of abating. Immigration is the definitive humanitarian issue of our age.

This poignant middle-grade story that reveals the dramatic story of a Muslim boy's banishment from his homeland could not be more timely and important.

In April of 1992, Kenan Trebincevic is a normal sports-obsessed 11-year-old living in Brčko, Bosnia. Although he doesn't go to the mosque every day like his grandma, he sees himself as a good Muslim. He tries to please his father, a popular sports trainer and his neatnik mother. When he asks why his grandmother is always kneeling on a rug, holding her prayer beads, his mom explains "We all go someplace to feel strong." For Kenan, that place is fudbal. He's thrilled on the perfect spring afternoon when he scores the winning goal in their match that gets the attention of Nina, the girl he has a crush on. It's Kenan's best day ever.

He has no idea why Nina—and all his Muslim friends—soon disappear.

In vivid detail, Kenan narrates the haunting saga of how soldiers swarm the local army base behind his school. Helicopters fly overhead. Armed trucks patrol the streets of his neighborhood. Fights break out between neighbors who have lived peacefully side-by-side: the Christian Orthodox Serbs, Catholic Croats and Bosnian Muslims, like him. Kenan watches in confusion as his nation divides into three rival teams.

He's hurt when his school friends turn on him, beat him up, and spit on him. He doesn't know how he became their enemy. Since Bosnia is surrounded on all sides by Serbia and Croatia, Kenan starts to realize they are in terrible danger. His uncle rushes his daughters to safety in Vienna, offering to take Kenan and Eldin too. But his father refuses. He's in denial, insisting this will all blow over. At first, Kenan believes him—until their city is being bombed. Running out to get bread for his family, Kenan bumps into his teacher Mr. Miran, now in uniform, who holds a gun to Kenan's head. Shocked and terrified, Kenan tries to figure out what he did wrong as Mr. Miran pulls the trigger. But his gun jams and Kenan escapes and races home.

A week later, Kenan's teacher Mr. Miran shows up at his doorstep with an AK-47, telling them they must "Leave or be killed!"

Where will they go?

Part One chronicles the family's failed escape attempts during the ten months they're prisoners in their own apartment, surrounded by armed Serbs who are now their enemy. The electricity and water shut off. They run out of food and Kenan is hungry every day. He can't bear to see dead dogs and cats lying outside abandoned restaurants, let alone Muslim corpses heaped onto meat trucks. When Kenan's father and brother are thrown into jail, Kenan prays they will survive. Thankfully they are released after two weeks. But they are still in danger, as their Serb neighbor steals clothes and furniture from Kenan's mother, threatening to turn them in to the Serb authorities. Kenan's mom keeps insisting there are good and bad in all types of people and someone will come to their rescue. But Kenan feels humiliated by their bad luck and loses his faith. He secretly makes a list of twelve people who have betrayed him and his family.

Almost a year into the war, a kind police officer—who coincidently also has the name of Kenan's teacher Mr. Miran—signs official papers so they can escape. Kenan thinks of him as "good Miran" balancing the betrayal of "bad Miran," his former teacher. On the harrowing 18-hour ride to meet his uncle in Vienna, Kenan's terrified the stone-faced Serbs on the bus will turn them in, sealing their death. But once they cross the border out of harm's way, the bus driver and passengers burst into applause, startling Kenan. Everyone wanted them to be safe. They have made it to freedom.

Part Two depicts problems Kenan's family faces as refugees in Vienna. Kenan loves the pastries they can afford to buy thanks to stipends from the Austrian government. But he struggles as one of eight relatives who sleep in the basement of his uncle's sister-in-law's Vienna house. They have no money to pay rent. With 100,000 refugees flooding the country, it's impossible to get citizenship. Kenan's mother babysits for a rich family. His father becomes a part-time gardener for an ambassador who helps Kenan's family apply for American citizenship. They're lucky to be sponsored by a council of churches and synagogues in Connecticut, though they never heard of the place before.

When Kenan's family lands in America, they are picked up at the airport by Don Hodges, a kind reverend. Having never met a Methodist before, Kenan is nervous. Don's Council members help them get jobs and donate furniture and clothes. A local Jewish doctor finds Kenan's mother has breast cancer and treats her for free. He's never met anyone Jewish either. An orthodontist gives Kenan braces to straighten his teeth for no charge. Kenan is amazed by all their kindness.

Still, Kenan's family are the only Muslims in town and barely speak broken English. While getting chemotherapy, his mother has to work full time as a data processor. His father slings chicken

The Book Bible

at a fast food restaurant and paints houses on weekends, before he gets a better job at a fruit cup factory. Eldin is a busboy at a local Mexican restaurant and sells knives door to door. Walking into his new sixth-grade classroom, Kenan feels like a mutt at the humane society, desperate to be adopted. He's embarrassed to be poor and friendless, with a funny accent. He's ashamed he doesn't know the language. He expects the kids will make fun of him.

Miguel, a small Spanish classmate, offers him a seat. He's impressed with the way Kenan plays the game his American friends call "soccer" in his new country. Miguel and his family take Kenan to Chicago where he sees his first professional soccer match. At a store where Miguel gets a flag from Spain, the salesman asks Kenan which team is his. "Was Yugoslavia, no more," he says, trying not to cry. Amid the international flags, Kenan spots the new Bosnian flag which he drapes around himself, feeling proud.

When Kenan joins a local soccer team, a Greek coach named Teddy Popadopoulos offers to drive him home when he needs rides. Kenan scores the winning goal of a championship game and feels the joy he's been missing for two years. Overcome with emotion and delight, he jumps on the back of Teddy, the first coach he's trusted since Mr. Miran turned on him.

At his mother's prompting, to counter the list he made of twelve betrayers, Kenan writes a new list, remembering twelve Serbs who actually helped them escape. He looks over the list and realizes that his family is actually one of the luckiest Muslim families in Bosnia because they didn't lose anyone. They all survived. Kenan has a loyal best friend in Miguel, and a coach he trusts. He begins to feel hopeful in his new life in America. His mother tells him: "We'll be nobodies in this country, so you and your brother can be somebodies someday."

World In Between: Based on a True Refugee Story is a riveting and timely narrative journey that traces one boy's heartbreaking story from being an innocent kid who hopes to get picked for soccer to a blacklisted refugee praying he won't be murdered by his teacher. Kenan shares his fear of being exiled from his homeland and then his gratitude towards a cross-section of Americans who treated his traumatized family with tolerance and kindness. It teaches young readers the universal lessons of love and generosity through one boy's hurt and healing, offering a powerful message about immigration, loss, forgiveness, and most of all hope.

This book can also show readers what they can do to help refugees—both locally and more generally through a list of resources we'll include in the back. Kenan also plans to write an afterword about all the wonderful things that happened to him in the United States—including getting his American citizenship and using his sports talent to become a physical therapist who can help others (as did his brother Eldin). Speaking out about being thrown out of his country and admitting that at twelve he'd "never even kissed a girl from home" led Kenan to love—when he went back to his former country and found a Bosnian bride. By looking back at his difficult past, he finds his future.

HERE'S *WORLD IN BETWEEN*'S SECTION ON COMPETITIVE AND COMPARABLE BOOK TITLES

We chose the following books, whether memoir or fictionalized narrative, because they told the first-person story of a protagonist much like ours—a child from a different country who loves their home and does not want to be uprooted or seen as different. Since this middle-grade nonfiction project was based on our adult coauthored memoir The Bosnia List, we picked books with similar origins.

It Ain't So Awful, Falafel by **Firoozeh Dumas (Clarion Books HMH, April 2017)** Also based on a Penguin Random House adult memoir

(*Funny in Farsi: A Memoir of Growing up Iranian in America*) aimed at ten- to twelve-year-old readers, this autobiographical middle-grade novel chronicles the story of an Iranian girl who left her homeland at 7 to move with her family to California in 1972. Similarly, *World In Between* chronicles the story of a non-practicing Muslim family's migration to the United States and illuminates an international political crisis while focusing on the loneliness of a foreign child desperate to fit in and understand why everything in their world is changing. Yet *World In Between* takes a darker, more realistic turn when Kenan's mother gets sick and his father keeps losing jobs. It better illuminates the pain of being a refugee at a time when immigration has become more dire and politicized.

***I Am Malala: My Story of Standing Up for Girls' Rights* by Malala Yousafzai and Sarah J. Robbins (Little, Brown Young Readers, October 2018) and *I Am Malala: How One Girl Stood Up for Education and Changed the World: Young Readers Edition* by Malala Yousafzai with Patricia McCormick (Hachette, August 2014)** These coauthored middle-grade memoirs by the Nobel Peace Prize winner were also based on an adult memoir. *I Am Malala* tells the story of a 15-year-old Muslim girl attacked by the Taliban, who takes over her town in Pakistan. When Malala refuses to be silenced, she's shot in the head while riding the bus home from school. *World In Between* centers on the Christian Orthodox Serb's ethnic cleansing campaign against Bosnian Muslims and includes scenes of Kenan at school. He's persecuted by his principal and his favorite teacher holds a gun to his head. Kenan is not injured, yet both books are inspirational stories of immigration. While Malala lives in England and Kenan is now in America, both narrators recently, triumphantly, went back to their homelands after their books came out. Though Malala has been interviewed by Oprah and is now a Noble Peace Prize winner, Kenan and his family still struggle in relative obscurity, which paints a more accurate picture of what migrants have to endure.

Between Shades of Gray by **Ruta Sepetys (Philomel, 2012)** When 15-year-old Lina Vilkas is arrested by the Soviet secret police and deported to Siberia with her mother and younger brother in 1939, she fights for her life. This bestselling novel—and movie—is also set in war time in Europe, in Lithuania. The author is the daughter of a Lithuanian refugee who based her novel on the true story of her relatives. Lina has difficulty accepting help from an enemy she's supposed to hate, and like Kenan, she struggles to keep her faith in mankind but in the end, succeeds. *World In Between* is told through a young male's point of view and is just as harrowing while sticking to a true story of ethnic cleansing that is reverberating today in China, Myanmar, and Kashmir.

Inside Out and Back Again by **Thanhha Lai (HarperCollins Children's Books, January 2013)** This award-winning bestselling novel about the Vietnam War tells a story similar to Kenan's, of a happy family being forced to leave their homeland (in this case, Saigon) through the eyes of a child. The author was 10 when her world was turned upside down. While moving to America means hope, she too struggles to fit into her strange new country. Told through a young boy's perspective, *World In Between* also illuminates a recent war. Like Kenan, Lai also now lives—and thrives—in New York. Yet what Kenan experienced was caused by nationalism and divided a country that never recovered, a cautionary tale especially relevant with the rise of nationalistic racism today.

Shooting Kabul by **N.H. Senzai (Paula Wiseman Books S and S, July, 2011)** This semi-autobiographical novel is set in 2001, when 12-year-old Fadi's parents and sister illegally leave Afghanistan and move to America. Based on the author's husband's experience fleeing Afghanistan in the 1970s, the book adds a very dramatic plot twist about Fadi's sister being left behind. Yet like *World In Between* it weaves international political unrest into an intimate narrative about a Muslim immigrant boy trying to leave his haunting past behind to adjust to his difficult new life in the United States. *World In Between* has more uplifting messages: by staying together, Kenan's family survived, and Americans of all backgrounds and religions came together to help Kenan and his relatives adjust to their new world.

***Zlata's Diary: A Child's Life in Wartime Sarajevo* by Zlata Filipovic (Penguin, 2006)** This bestselling cross-marketed memoir, compared to *The Diary of Anne Frank*, centers around a typical 11-year-old girl, Zlata, who is preoccupied by school and birthday parties, when the Balkan War hits her Bosnian hometown in 1992. Like Kenan, she's used to being comfortable in a loving, middle-class family and struggles with the lack of food and electricity and the disappearance of close friends. She doesn't understand the complicated ethnic struggles during the breakup of Yugoslavia. Zlata also settled abroad (in Dublin) and now visits her hometown as an author. *World In Between* offers a more realistic prose-driven narrative of survival with a history lesson warning against the kind of nationalistic politics now repeating themselves all over the world.

HERE ARE SUMMARIES OF THE FIRST TWO AND LAST TWO CHAPTERS

Chapter One: Kenan is thrilled when his favorite teacher Mr. Miran chooses him to play in a fifth-grade fudbal game one April recess in Brčko, his Yugoslavian hometown. At 11, he hates being called "Bugs" and "Chicken Arms" for his bad teeth and skinny limbs. He wants to be as good an athlete as his annoying 17-year-old brother Eldin. Kenan hopes to impress his teacher and Nina, the coolest girl in his class. He's ecstatic to score the winning goal. It's March 1992, and he doesn't understand why everything is changing around him. Soldiers have started to swarm the army base behind the school. Army helicopters roar overhead. Kenan is from a close-knit Muslim family; his dad and uncle were in the army reserves, so he isn't worried. Then he overhears his parents arguing about political divisions between Catholic

Croatians, Christian Orthodox Serbs and Bosnian Muslims like him. "It won't affect us," his Dad says. "This is our home. Everyone here likes us." Kenan believes his father, who is always right about everything.

Chapter Two: When Eldin goes to a fudbal game in Croatia, their mother Adisa worries when she hears of political riots breaking out between rival fans. A train station on his way home is bombed. The Serbs in their neighborhood fly a new red double-headed eagle flag. Kenan's mom sees strange men in dark uniforms lurking around. Kenan is confused when his best friends Victor, Ivan and Marko only want Serbs like them to play on their team. Kenan notices his Muslim classmates are disappearing and he worries when Nina and her sister's seats are empty at school.

Chapter Twenty-Eight: Kenan's nice history teacher in Norwalk, Connecticut helps him start doing better in his new American school. But Kenan worries he'll have to quit his soccer team because his parents don't have a car and the soccer moms can't always take him. His giant Greek coach Teddy Popadopoulos offers to drive Kenan from now on. He's glad but can't help but feel skeptical, flashing back to his Bosnian teacher Mr. Miran, holding a gun to his head.

Chapter Twenty-Nine: During the championship game of his Connecticut soccer team, Kenan scores the winning goal. He feels joy for the first time in two years since the war started. He runs over to his coach Teddy and jumps on his back as they all celebrate. Between his new coach, best friend Miguel, and the kind people of all religions and backgrounds who've helped his family, Kenan gives up the fantasy of moving back to his homeland—which is still at war. He starts to thrive in America, his new home.

EXPERT ADVICE ON NONFICTION PROPOSALS

I always love having Paul Whitlatch on my panels. A fellow NYU alum, he's worked at Simon and Schuster, Norton and Hachette Book Group. We met when he edited my former student David Goodwillie's acclaimed debut novel *American Subversive* (2010) and I impolitely noted that Whitlatch, in his early twenties, seemed ridiculously young to be such a publishing big shot. He soon became more known as a nonfiction editor of bestsellers and award-winning books like Jennifer Percy's *Demon Camp: The Strange and Terrible Saga of a Soldier's Return from War* (2015), Liza Mundy's *Code Girls: The Untold Story of the American Women Code Breakers of World War II* (2017), Tom Wright and Bradley Hope's *Billion Dollar Whale: The Man Who Fooled Wall Street, Hollywood, and the World* (2018) and Anne Glenconner's *Lady In Waiting* (2020). Now, as an executive editor at Crown (and still ridiculously young), he acquires and edits books spanning current events, history, popular science, business and politics, all bought from proposals. So I asked him for the inside scoop of what would make him bid on a nonfiction book being proposed.

1. **Beautifully Craft Your Proposal:** Many people try to sell books in the dry way they would pitch a business proposition. Yet the most compelling projects showcase lyrical prose that soars off the page. Even if you're proposing a political treatise, show flashes of lively writing, dazzling dialogue and riveting scenes, peppering in the kind of idiosyncratic details that stay with readers. Some people working on memoirs finish most of their manuscript, then use the best sections for their proposal.

2. **Make Your Overview Overwhelmingly Vivid:** This first section is the most important part, Whitlatch says. It shouldn't be perfunctory or mechanical. Write it in the engaging voice and style of your book. For memoirs and other narrative-based nonfiction, it's especially important to showcase a strong, confident voice from the first sentence that draws readers in, creates intrigue and dares them to keep turning pages. Editors get inundated with submissions. If they aren't hooked by the first page—or paragraph—of the overview, they might not keep reading.

3. **Present a Strong Case for Your Project:** In proposing your book, you have to win over an editor on two fronts: the author and the

market. Most nonfiction is platform-driven. So the sample pages need to prove the writer has the chops to excite people to cough up money for the book. But no matter how talented or innovative the work, you also have to build a persuasive argument that the author's perch in the world and existing notoriety/network will translate into a huge audience.

4. **Getting Recent Comp Titles Is Good for You:** To make an offer on a book project, most mainstream publishers run an "acquisition P and L." That's a projection of how much money a book stands to earn if it performs according to the (generally rosy) sales track the editor envisions. To make this document compelling, it models sales data on comparative titles, previously published books that are similar to the one being pitched. But editors are only allowed to use books that were published in the previous two to three years, since they better reflect the current sales environment. So if you want to make it more likely that you'll get a deal, spend a lot of time finding fresh comp titles. Also check Publishers Marketplace to make sure somebody didn't sell a book project with the exact same premise a month ago.

5. **Keep It Short and Simple:** Whitlatch admits that he's jumped out of his chair after reading an amazing 30-page proposal just as often as one that stretches 100 pages. Don't waste time throat-clearing or telling editors obvious things about the book market in your genre. (Like: political books are hot now.) Assume editors reading your proposal are intelligent, with strong bullshit detectors. And unless you're writing a proposal for a design- or illustration-heavy book, don't obsess about fonts, photos or other bells and whistles. Don't separate the proposal and sample chapters into multiple files. No editor wants the headache of an email with multiple attachments.

6. **Listen to Experts in Your Field:** Book publishing is a collaborative art. Don't write in a vacuum and rush your project to editors and agents, convinced it's your way or the highway. Get feedback first and consider the criticism carefully. But make sure it's from editors,

agents or authors who've sold similar proposals and therefore know the market. (I remember once getting advice on my memoir from a brilliant poet that was completely off-base. Luckily, it's only bad advice if you take it.)

7. **Your Proposal Can Differ Radically from Your Finished Book:** Remember, a proposal is just an outline and blueprint of the book that will grow from it. So don't flip out if you're not positive how it will end or consider all the compartments complete or etched in stone. Be open to compromise and making changes based on ongoing dialogue with your editor.

   There are many kinds of nonfiction books that you can sell with a proposal that include the elements I just mentioned. Here's specific suggestions for how to slant your proposal for different popular subcategories of factual books.

ADVICE ABOUT ESSAY COLLECTIONS FROM AN ESSAYIST

After my former student Sarah Gerard sold two beautifully crafted essays to the *New York Times* and *New York Magazine,* I wasn't surprised she was publishing an acclaimed essay collection *Sunshine State* (Harper Perennial, 2017), revolving around her Florida hometown. It received two *New York Times* raves and was on Best Nonfiction Book of the Year lists by NPR, *Vanity Fair, BuzzFeed* and *Nylon.* She's also published two novels, *Binary Star* (2015) and *True Love* (2020), and has taught writing at NYU, Columbia University, Sarah Lawrence and New College of Florida. From a writer's perspective, here's what she recommends with essays.

1. **Embrace Thoughtful Feedback:** There are many ways to find helpful criticism, whether it's from teachers and fellow students in your MFA program (Gerard studied at The New School), or you get help from a mentor for free, join a weekly writing workshop, or hire a ghost editor. She has found literary critiques on a regular

basis to be enlightening. While she only takes the advice that rings true, Gerard finds that the continual human connection really helps her keep going.

2. **Submit Work to Publications You Admire:** Gerard reads a lot of different newspapers, magazines and literary journals. She was impressed with the interviews, arts coverage and cultural pieces in *Bomb* magazine and *The Brooklyn Rail*, so she started submitting her own pieces there. She later expanded her repertoire by contributing to *Granta*, *The Baffler*, *Vice*, *Bookforum* and *The Paris Review*.

3. **Save Everything:** Sometimes, if a piece or a book isn't working, Gerard puts it away and returns to it at a later date. She's currently revisiting two books that she began but abandoned ten years ago and now has better ideas on how to complete them. "I'm so glad I have all of this documented but didn't try to publish them earlier," she said.

4. **Don't Be Afraid to Geek Out:** While some of the eight essays in her book are personal narratives, Gerard also enjoys history, researching and reporting. In one piece, she combined all of them by interviewing her mother about her childhood church. When in doubt, learn something new.

5. **Weave in Multiple Themes:** Although her collection is externally set near Tampa Bay where she grew up, Gerard simultaneously unraveled her own personal mysteries involving drugs, faith, friendship and her early life as an artist. Gerard also kept in mind the overriding intellectual question: What does it mean to believe something is true? Although it's good to have a central focus, an essay collection doesn't have to only be about one thing.

6. **Mix Genres:** Gerard writes novels, short stories, poetry and essays and enjoys experimenting with different forms—sometimes in the same essay. After an agent asked if she could expand her *New York Times* piece—about an eating disorder and suicidal feelings—into a memoir, she was too scared. So she turned it into a novel, which was easier for her to complete. "Whatever keeps you writing," she says.

7. **Be Open for Feedback**: The agent agreed to handle her novel—if Gerard would next try an essay collection. Yet the first draft of her proposal didn't sell because, some editors felt, all the separate essays weren't quite gelling thematically. For the second draft, Gerard responded to their notes by setting all the pieces in Florida and calling it *Sunshine State,* which made it more cohesive and salable.

ADVICE ABOUT ESSAY COLLECTIONS FROM A RANDOM HOUSE EDITOR

Reading through the *Publishers Weekly* "Star Watch" Honoree list last year, I noticed a twenty-something recent City College of New York graduate, Amber Oliver. After an internship with Akashic Books and roles at InkWell Management and Glitterati Inc., it said the Bronx native was already an assistant editor at HarperCollins, acquiring both fiction and nonfiction that uplifted marginalized voices. I asked her to be a panelist at an NYU event, where my students were inspired by her enthusiasm, and her wish list of the kind of manuscripts she's looking for: humor, LGBTQ, pop culture, feminism, social justice and especially her excitement for essay collections, which have become more popular of late.

Indeed, her list features Morgan Jerkins, author of the recent *Wandering in Strange Lands: A Daughter of the Great Migration Reclaims Her Roots*, and previously *This Will Be My Undoing: Living at the Intersection of Black, Female and Feminist in (White) America*, along with Shayla Lawson, who wrote *This Is Major: Notes on Diana Ross, Dark Girls and Being Dope* (2020). Before her author Ben Phillipe's memoir-in-essays *Sure I'll Be Your Black Friend: Notes from the Other Side of the Fist Bump* even came out in 2021, Oliver was promoted to a Penguin Random House editorship, where she'll buy books for their Dutton, Tiny Reparations, Plume and Berkeley imprints. Here's an editor's take on what's important for an essay collection.

1. **Get a Theme:** Whether it's a hot-button issue like #MeToo, race, gender, politics, illness or feminism, each essay in your collection

should be a piece to the same puzzle the reader is putting together. Read award-winning essays in Hilton Al's *White Girls* (2013), Eula Bliss's *On Immunity* (2014), Rebecca Solnit's *The Mother of All Questions* (2017), Valeria Luiselli's *Tell Me How It Ends* (2017), Ta-Nehisi Coates's *We Were Eight Years in Power* (2017), Sarah Gerard's *Sunshine State* (2017), Esmé Weijun Wang's *The Collected Schizophrenias* (2019) or Bassey Ikpi's *I'm Telling the Truth But I'm Lying* (2019). Notice how these authors weave their theme throughout. Ask yourself: What is my book really about? Come up with an evocative title, subtitle, issue or argument that your work illuminates.

2. **Research the Right Editors and Agents:** Not everyone handles essay collections. The quickest route to rejection is sending someone a manuscript in a genre they don't work in. If you Google well, you will learn that Oliver is *not* interested in science fiction or historical novels, romance, erotica, young adult, middle-grade, fantasy or screenplays. Many writers depend on their literary agency to figure this out, but it's not a bad idea to do your own research. Attend conferences or panels to find who is doing what with essays. But don't assume the editors who published Ali Wong's *Dear Girls* (2019) or Zadie Smith's *Intimations: Six Essays* (2020) will want your book, even if it's similar. Don't compare yourself to famous authors, and make sure the editors you target are open to debut writers who aren't well known.

3. **Be Ready to Revise:** While writing is solitary, editing and publishing is collaborative and you should embrace criticism. First, show your material to teachers or beta readers and listen to their reaction. Listen to feedback you're getting from agents. Even after you sell your book, expect comments and suggestions from your editor, marketing, publicity and the sales department too. Before making an offer on a book, Oliver will sometimes speak to the author to make sure they share the same vision and are willing to rewrite. If you're not, you can self-publish, she said. If you want a top-five publisher, it's a community where you have to be a team player.

4. **Know How to Position Your Book:** Pick realistic comparative titles that have come out within the last five years, but not mega-hits that sold millions of copies by TV stars like Tina Fey, Mindy Kaling and Lena Dunham. For example, Shayla Lawson's essays on the richness and resilience of Black girl culture were aimed at readers of the essayists Samantha Irby, Lindy West, Morgan Jenkins and Roxane Gay. Accurate comparison titles arm agents and editors with the language and labels needed to convince the publisher's marketing forces to take a chance on you.

5. **Share an Eclectic Author Bio:** Along with where you've been published or went to school, consider adding your occupation, where you live, where you're from and idiosyncratic personal details. On Goodreads it says that Ben Phillipe was born in Haiti, raised in Montreal, is now based in New York and is a graduate of UT Austin and Columbia University who "still doesn't have a valid driver's license, which is both #beautiful and #brave." Shayla Lawson's bio says she's a poet who grew up in Kentucky and set down roots in its poetry slam scene before majoring in architecture at the University of Kentucky. Make yourself sound fascinating, the kind of person an editor would want to learn more about.

6. **Most Essays Should Be New:** Only famous or previously bestselling authors get to collect all of their published pieces in a book. When you're less known, you have to do more work. If there are ten essays in your collection, only two should already be published and included in the proposal. But at least 80 percent of the material should be fresh and unpublished (that includes posted on social media).

7. **A Platform Is Important:** You don't have to be a celebrity to get a book deal, but it helps to be happening in your field. Phillipe, who teaches at Barnard, has written for *Vanity Fair, The Guardian, Observer* and *Playboy*. Jerkins, who teaches at Columbia University, is a senior editor at ZORA and her work has appeared in *The New Yorker, Rolling Stone* and *Esquire*. Teaching at a reputable school, publishing short pieces, or amassing social media followers shows

an editor that you're capable of commanding an audience who will—hopefully—all rush to buy your book.

EXPERT ADVICE ON COOKBOOKS

How does pitching a cookbook, lifestyle project or design hardcover differ from other nonfiction proposals? I asked Martha Hopkins, a literary agent and cofounder of Terrace Partners, a boutique agency and book development company in Austin, Texas. She got her start as an author herself, selling 325,000 copies of *Intercourses: An Aphrodisiac Cookbook*, appearing on *Good Morning America*, CNN and the TV Food Network. She's since worked on many food and lifestyle books, including *Black Girl Baking* by Jerrelle Guy, *United Tastes of Texas* by Jessica Dupuy, *Spruce Upholstery* by Amanda Brown and *The Last Stop: Vanishing Rest Stops of the American Roadside* by Jesse Griffiths. Is it still possible to break into this crowded arena, where you have to compete with everyone from Gordon Ramsay to Padma Lakshmi to Chrissy Teigen? According to Hopkins, here's your best bet.

1. **Find a Fresh, Multi-faceted Idea:** While it's hard to imagine a book on mayonnaise doing well, Ashley Strickland Freeman's *The Duke's Mayonnaise Cookbook: 75 Recipes Celebrating the Perfect Condiment* (2020) was a hit. It includes a personal intro, the back story of the South Carolina–based company, along with recipes and testimonials from chefs across the country. Tony Tipton-Martin used her investigative reporting skills for *Jubilee: Recipes from Two Centuries of African American Cooking* (2019), incorporating cooking secrets with a celebration of Black chefs long forgotten and Black culinary history. In *Drinking with Chickens: Free-Range Cocktails for the Happiest Happy Hour* (2020), Kate E. Richards offers unusual cocktails—some with egg whites—with pictures of her chicken-filled California house and garden, fun fowls photo-bombing every shot. (And Hopkins's own first idea for *Intercourses*, which had a sexy red and white cover, was aimed at Valentine's Day and

featured romantic foods. It had four elements going for it: dazzling title, sexy design, engaging content that connected with the cover, and a timely marketing angle.)

2. **Up Your Platform:** Color printing and photography for these books can be so expensive that publishers want to mitigate their financial risks by making sure you have a receptive audience. Increasing your social media connections can help. Jessica Siskin's Instagram photos of Rice Krispies Treat sculptures led to her book *Treat Yourself* (2017), which landed her on *The Today Show*. And like most other writing fields, publishing short pieces can earn you payment and prominence. (Get clips from *Grub Street, Eater, Bon Appétit, Feast, Taste, Edibles, Rachael Ray* and *New Food* magazines, along with Food and Life newspaper sections.)

3. **Fact-Check and Taste Test:** Many editors and agents buying a cookbook and those judging cookbook contests—including Hopkins—will try out your recipes to test their veracity. Make sure they'll be able to recreate your masterpieces at home—perfectly. If you're worried, you can hire a tester for a practice run. Good to get the kinks out early since, if you're lucky, you could be asked to make your recipe on a television or video cooking segment.

4. **Find Who Is Missing:** If you don't have a big name yet, connect with someone who does. Food celebrities need coauthors, as chef Joshua McFadden collaborated with Martha Holmberg for *Six Seasons,* and David Boulud worked with Sylvie Bigar. Early in her career, cookbook aficionado Melissa Clark coauthored *Sylvia's Family Soul Cookbook: From Hemingway, South Carolina to Harlem* (1999) with the restaurant's owner Sylvia Woods. (Working with a star may only earn you a set fee, not a percentage of the advance or royalties, but it can be a great stepping stone.) Or ask someone well known to pen your foreword or intro, as Catherine Deneuve did for Bigar's *Living Art: Style Your Home with Flowers*. Their fee is sometimes paid by the publisher, though it might come from the author's advance, as does the payment for photography.

5. **Know Your Market:** Saying "I want to do a vegan cookbook" is way too general at this point. You need a clear plan and distinct audience. My former student Leah Koenig, a young Jewish food journalist, played up kosher recipes from her childhood in *The Hadassah Everyday Cookbook: Daily Meals for the Contemporary Jewish Kitchen* (2011), *Modern Jewish Cooking* (2015), *Little Book of Jewish Appetizers* (2017), *Little Book of Jewish Feasts* (2018), *Little Book of Jewish Sweets* (2019), *The Jewish Cookbook* (2019) and *Roman Jewish Cooking* (2021). Illyanna Maisonet, the first US Puerto Rican food columnist whose *San Francisco Chronicle* column explored disappearing Puerto Rican recipes, also wrote for *Food and Wine, Lucky Peach, Paste, East Bay Express, Food* and her own newsletter and blog *EatGordaEat*. She recently announced on Twitter that she's sold her debut book *Diasporican: A Puerto Rican Cookbook* (2022).

6. **Go Small and Specialize:** Sometimes specificity is more universal and smarter for marketing. Instead of covering the food of the most diverse New York borough, authors John Wang and Storm Garner focused on one literal market in *The World Eats Here: Amazing Food and the Inspiring People Who Make It at New York's Queens Night Market* (2020). My colleague, wine critic Alice Feiring, centered on just organic wines in *Naked Wine* (2011) and *Natural Wine for the People* (2019).

7. **Three's Company:** If there's a specific food, chef, baker, caterer or restaurant you admire, pitch a story on them to a local publication, then ask to join forces for a book. Between chefs, authors, photographers and restaurant owners, byline trios on cookbooks are common. Yes, you have to share the money, but also the workload and acclaim. *Dishoom: The First Ever Cookbook from the Much-Loved Indian Restaurant* (2019) author credits include the founder cousins Shamil and Kavi Thakrar with chef Naved Nasir. Having several names on the cover of a novel or poetry collection is rare, yet cookbooks don't necessarily mind the companionship.

SECTION TWO
SHORTER BOOKS

CHAPTER 5

Poetry

HOW *NOT* TO PUBLISH POETRY

1. **Complete a Poem in Twenty-Four Hours:** Race to get down your entire stream of consciousness, considering your first draft the finished product.
2. **Refuse to Edit:** Since your initial thoughts are the freshest and most honest, don't risk ruining the rawness by revising.
3. **Make Sure You Rhyme:** Every single time. Since rhyming is sublime. And will help you make a dime.
4. **Ignore All Criticism:** You know what you're trying to say. Not your problem if your teachers, classmates and editors can't comprehend the breadth of your brilliant creation.
5. **Avoid All Other Poets and Their Events:** That way, you won't be influenced by anybody else's voice and can focus on your own. Why celebrate others' acclaim when nobody is paying any attention to you? That'll show 'em.
6. **Send All Your New Work to *The New Yorker*:** Instead of submitting one polished poem, submit a series of twenty, or an early draft of your whole book so the editors can pick the ones they love best.
7. **Be Impatient:** Have a fit when you don't hear back from editors you don't know after a month. The whole system is rigged towards people who are better connected than you are anyway.

8. **Self-Publish:** Since no editor is getting back to you, get your poems out there quickly, ignoring all the usual channels and pay all the costs yourself. You'll make your money back in no time.

9. **Quit Your Day Job:** Though most poets have to teach to make a living, they aren't as talented or dedicated as you are. Dump your boring 9 to 5 grind until you make it big.

10. **Forget All Other Genres:** Be pure to your craft, forgetting that most poets also publish essays, reviews, critical studies and even fiction.

BETTER PATH TO PUBLISHING POETRY

There is no money in poetry. The only reason to write it is for love—or possibly to learn literary dexterity or gain prestige in certain artistic circles. I need to get that out of the way since the word "sell" is in my subtitle and I wouldn't want you harboring the illusion that your book of poems will earn a million dollars. If it did during your lifetime, yours might be the first. Walt Whitman's collection of brave free verse *Leaves of Grass,* said to bridge the gap between realism and transcendentalism, couldn't even find an editor. So in 1855, he self-published it, failing to find a big audience. He kept revising and it only became a bestseller after his 1892 death. Sylvia Plath's dark, confessional, lyrically astute *Ariel* (1965) also became a blockbuster posthumously.

I am not denigrating poetry for not being lucrative. I want to clarify the difference in genres that took me so long to grasp. In the decade I spent passionately writing and publishing poems, the most I ever earned was $100 from *Cosmopolitan* and $50 from a well-known journal that took two years to come out. After toiling on a collection for a dozen years, I was paid a $500 advance from a tiny press and considered myself lucky to find a publisher. It's not a case of sour grapes (excuse the cliché, a poetry no-no) because I'm a failed poet. As the late British poet Robert Graves quipped, "There's no money in poetry, but then there's no poetry in money either."

Historically, collections of poems that paid off in the United States were humorous rhyming light verse. Satirist Dorothy Parker, founding member of the Algonquin Round Table and *The New Yorker* staff writer, hit big with her debut *Enough Rope* (1926), selling 47,000 copies. It contained her famous poem, *Résumé*. Though the *New York Times* critic sniffed that it was "flapper verse," Parker found more success as a critic, theatre writer and Oscar-nominated screenwriter for such films as *A Star Is Born*.

Ogden Nash's *Hard Lines* (1931) also debuted in *The New Yorker* (then a chattier, funnier magazine under editor Harold Ross). That led to seven printings, national recognition and five more collections.

Following the funny train were Judith Viorst's bestselling light verse, *It's Hard to Be Hip Over Thirty* (1968) and *People and Other Aggravations* (1971).

More successful was Rod McKuen's pop poetry that sold 60 million copies, with lyrics like "It's nice sometimes/to open up the heart a little/ and let some hurt come in." A songwriter, he won a Grammy award, was nominated for Oscars and a Pulitzer for his music compositions, and promoted child advocacy, LGBT rights and AIDS charities. Yet poetry critics and academics called his work "uniformly vituperative" and "sweet kitsch."

Since 2014, an Abu Dhabi–based You've Got Talent–type TV show called *Millions Poet* rewards seven-figure prizes for the best self-penned verses recited in Nabati form, colloquial Arabic. Some have been political and revolutionary, as when a Saudi Arabian mother of four in full niqab won third prize for a poem criticizing her own country's religious edicts. So far, poetry TV shows have not caught on in America.

Clearly, most poets need another way to pay their bills. In "Poet's Odd Jobs," the Academy of American Poets lists early professions of Maya Angelou (streetcar conductor), T.S. Eliot (banker), Lucille Clifton (claims clerk), Langston Hughes (busboy), Wallace Stevens (insurance lawyer), Williams Carlos Williams (doctor), Anne Sexton (model), Robert Frost (light trimmer), Charles Bukowski (postal clerk), Edna St.

Vincent Millay (actress), Allen Ginsberg (ship storekeeper) and Walt Whitman (nurse, government clerk journalist and teacher).

You could aspire to be a US Poet Laureate like luminaries Rita Dove, Phillip Levin, Louise Glück, Stanley Kunitz, Tracy K. Smith and Juan Felipe Herrera. Joy Harjo, a member of the Muscogee/Creek Nation, was granted a second term 2020–2021. There is a $35,000 annual stipend, plus $5,000 for travel, and there have only been twenty-three since the Library of Congress established it in 1985. Forty-four states have an official state poet laureate, a job created in 2005 that pays $2,500 to $10,000. Some cities have their own. Brooklyn has had four poet laureates. That gig offers between $500 and $2,500 for a year term, according to Poets.org.

There are multiple grants and awards given for excellence in the field. Yet Pulitzer Prize–winning poet Galway Kinnell, my NYU professor, confided that the poets he knew, even famous ones, taught to make a living. He couldn't support his family without teaching (until his eighties) even after he won a 1984 MacArthur Fellowship for $300,000 at fifty-seven, for his six lauded collections.

To get more up-to-date, I spoke with Deborah Garrison, the poetry editor at Knopf, one of the top publishers in the world. We first met working at *The New Yorker* right out of college. I was jealous she sold a poem to Howard Moss, then poetry editor, in 1987. It was thirteen lines and the magazine paid $20 a line so she earned $260, an astronomically high fee for a poem then. Her 1998 debut Random House book *A Working Girl Can't Win* sold 30,000 copies, a poetry bestseller that garnered royalties. It received accidental crossover energy from that moment of *Sex and the City* and other "working girl" explorations in popular culture, which propelled it beyond the usual poetry audience. Her second book in 2007, *The Second Child*, which many believed was artistically stronger, sold fewer copies. That's the paradox of publishing—you can never determine what will be a hit. Some books find a windfall due to their relationship with the zeitgeist or their sheer overwhelming quality. Others might be wonderful but completely missed by the culture. Or by an editor.

After a change of editorship, *The New Yorker* didn't take Garrison's poems for a decade—until a different poetry editor came aboard, loved her work, and published more, underscoring how subjective poetry—or any publication—is. It reminds me of how I once tried the *New York Times Magazine* humor column Endpaper with "Quitters Never Win," about going insane my first day after quitting cigarettes. The editor Jim said no. After fourteen more tries and rejections, I asked an older friend there where I should try next. "Endpaper," he said.

"I tried them first, they said no."

"You tried Jim? He left and a new editor named Penelope took over. She's young and kooky just like you and she's trying to quit smoking."

I sent the piece back to the first place I tried, where the new editor bought it. That led to my Random House memoir. Quitters Never Win, indeed. I recalled a party thrown by my mentor Harvey, filled with major poets I admired, right after I'd sent him the galley and confided to him that it earned a $50,000 advance. Harvey had once told me he feared my poems had "too many words, not enough music." I was embarrassed that I'd switched genres, fearing the old gang would think I'd sold out. Walking in, there was a round of applause. When I asked him why, he said, "There's more poetry in your prose than in your poems. And we only get $1,000 for a poetry book." I was shocked.

"Poetry advances are usually in the $1,000 to $4,000 range now," Garrison confirmed. "And Knopf rarely publishes someone's first collection. Most of our poets have books out from smaller presses before we take them on. If authors earn out their advances, the number goes up to reflect what they can earn. But I don't think any of us measure poetry success in those terms. Neither the publishers nor the poets are making a killing. But it's a joy to publish strong, lasting work in book form. And poetry *pays* over time as it becomes part of the canon, and is anthologized and passed down. While individual books may not sell a lot initially, some poems or whole collections become permanent with time."

I thought of Langston Hughes's 1951 poem *Harlem*: "What happens to a dream deferred/Does it dry up/like a raisin in the sun?/Or fester like a sore-/And then run?/Does it stink like rotten meat?/Or crust and sugar over-/like a syrupy sweet?/Maybe it just sags/like a heavy load./Or does it explode?" Those 52 words in eleven lines still epitomize the culture seven decades later. It remains one of the most influential poems of the 20th century and inspiration for another classic, Lorraine Hansberry's play *A Raisin in the Sun.*

While I'm old school and consider poetry to be literary verse published on the page, there's recent variations like rap music, hip hop and performance poems associated with oral traditions and the spoken word, meant to be performed by the author. This was popularized at New York's Nuyorican Poets Cafe, founded in 1973. I loved their poetry slams, introduced by Bob Holman and Miguel Algarin in 1988, continued at the Bowery Poetry Club. Performance poetry reached a larger audience between 2002 and 2007 with Russell Simmons' Def Poetry on HBO. And I know someone who made money from advertisers to their poetry blog, though it's easier to garner praise than payment from blogging.

In the social media trend of Insta-poetry, young poets have found it feasible to post their sometimes mixed media work on Twitter, Instagram, Facebook, Tumblr, Medium and YouTube. Indian-born Canadian poet Rupi Kaur, 28, who writes about love, heartbreak and womanhood, has 4 million Instagram followers. Her debut collection *Milk and Honey* came out from indie publisher Andrews McMeel in 2015, hitting the *New York Times* bestseller list by selling 2 million copies (according to Wikipedia, 3 million and *The Atlantic* 3.5, noting she outsold Homer's *The Odyssey*). It has been translated into thirty languages. Her second collection *The Sun and Her Flowers* came out in 2017 from the same publisher.

Her fame rose in 2015 when she posted a shot of herself on Instagram lying in bed with her back to the camera, menstrual blood leaking through her sweatpants. Instagram removed the image twice for breaking community guidelines. She claimed censorship, according to *Rolling Stone*. "Their patriarchy is leaking. Their misogyny is leaking. We will not be censored," wrote her Facebook post, shared over eighteen thousand times. Her letter went viral, Instagram apologized, and an internet star was born.

The Atlantic chronicled her rise in a technology piece "How Instagram Saved Poetry: Social media is turning an art form into an industry." Yet like McKuen and other non-academic poets, Kaur's work has been called superficial and simplistic by critics. She was accused by poet Nayyirah Waheed of plagiarism, a charge she denied. Parody accounts showed up on Twitter. *BuzzFeed* criticized her for using collective women's trauma and Rebecca Watts published *The Cult of the Noble Amateur* in *Poetry Nation's* online magazine, reiterating the old trope that "artless poetry sells," and decrying its "open denigration of intellectual engagement and rejection of craft."

That could be true of provocative poet/stand-up comic/chanteuse Catherine Cohen, whose sharp, funny poetry book *God I Feel Modern Tonight: Poems for a Gal About Town* was published by Garrison at Knopf in 2021. Cohen posted funny songs and poems on YouTube, and last I checked she had more than 61,000 followers on Twitter and Instagram, a podcast and was on Seth Meyers's TV show.

Like McKuen, there continues to be crossover between music and poetry. Grammy-nominated American singer Halsey published a Simon and Schuster collection of poems called "I Would Leave Me if I Could." Bridging the gap between her painting, performing, singing and songwriting, this book will explore her "doomed relationships, family ties, sexuality and mental illness," her press release said, calling her work "more hand-grenades than confessions." Songwriter Lana Del Rey also questions her feminism in her upcoming audio poetry book *Violet Bent Backwards Over the Grass*.

Performance poetry, songwriters' lyrics and Insta-poems have yet to be taken seriously by the mainstream poetry powers that be. Yet how you write, use and publish your verse depends on your personal goals.

And as my rule goes with love and writing: "You can do anything as long as it works."

TO BE A PUBLISHED POET, TRY THIS

1. **Be a Poetry Junkie:** Keep up with collections, anthologies, magazines and journals that publish poems like *The American Poetry Review, Poetry East, The Paris Review, Ploughshares* and *The Kenyon Review*. This way you'll know where to submit your work. *Poets and Writers* has listings for poetry submissions you can try and grants to apply for. Sign up for the Poetry Foundation's free digital Poem-a-Day series to be inspired by a poet reading their work aloud.

2. **Go to Readings:** Check out local bookstore and college listings for public events to attend. You can often speak with the poet afterwards (especially if you ask them to sign their book), as well as meet their editor and cohorts. Make friends with other aspiring poets and learn about free workshops and open mic opportunities you can get involved with.

3. **Be a Follower:** Many poets are on Facebook and Twitter. I follow: Kevin Young (@deardarkness), Rita Dove (@rita_Dove5B), Billie Collins (@bcollinspoetry), Caroline Forche (@carolineforche), Sharon Olds (@old_Sharon), Deborah Landau (@landaudeborah) and Juan Felipe Herrera (@cilantroman). It's thrilling to see what they're writing, promoting and thinking, where they're reading, and to make contact directly. I also enjoy Tracey K. Smith's podcast slowdownshow.org with @poetryfound.

4. **Support Poetry Groups:** If you want poetic opportunities to flourish, help it. Join Poetry Society of America, Association of Writers and Writing Programs, Academy of American Poets, Poetry Foundation, Poet's House or Poetry Project. Contribute to associations that support and award poetry like PEN American Center, National Book Awards and National Book Critics Circle. Often you can attend festivals and conferences for a small fee or none, or

get a scholarship. I once went to a free NBCC reading and sat next to one of my poetry idols, Adrienne Rich.

5. **Take Poetry Classes:** If you can afford it, get an MFA to improve your poems by studying with luminaries you admire and class-mates for community, connections and support. If not, take one course with a poet you admire. I noticed former Poet Laureate Billy Collins teaches a MasterClass online.

6. **Hire a Poetry Editor:** Since, as I mentioned, poetry is not a big money-making profession, many well-published poets will give private lessons, instruction or do one-to-one coaching or edit-ing. Having a mentor or guru to give you honest feedback could enhance your work immeasurably.

7. **Submit Poems to Magazines, Journals and Calls for Work for Anthologies:** While *The New Yorker* remains the Holy Grail, tons of small poetry magazines, webzines and journals take new poets. If you follow #3 closely, you'll know which editors take work that's closest to yours. Start your cover letter mentioning you're a sub-scriber and quoting your recent favorite. The more great poems you publish in prestigious journals, the more likely you'll find a publisher for your book-length manuscript.

8. **Put Together a Collection:** Though I had tons of poems scattered in notebooks and school magazines, it was an illuminating exercise to put them all together and try to figure out a sequence, title and subtitle. I even made the cover to envision what I wanted it to be. And then I found a small press who took it.

9. **Enter Contests for Chapbooks and First Books:** I loved Natalie Diaz's collection *When My Brother Was an Aztec,* which won pub-lication from Copper Canyon Press in 2012. That led to major awards and fellowships that launched her career.

10. **Try a Wide Range of Book Editors:** Once you've published indi-vidual poems and a first book with smaller houses, be brave and submit to major publishers' imprints like Norton, Knopf, FSG and Penguin, as well as such smaller places like Dzanc, Hanging Loose,

Coffee House and Copper Canyon presses. It's one of the few arenas where you don't need an agent.

EXPERT ADVICE

Here are seven pieces of advice from the award-winning poet Grace Schulman. She's the author of eight acclaimed poetry collections including *The Marble Bed* (Turtle Point Press, 2020), *Without a Claim* (Mariner Books, 2013) and *The Broken String* (Houghton Mifflin, 2007), as well as the memoir *Strange Paradise* (Turtle Point Press, 2018) and *Marianne Moore: The Poetry of Engagement* (Paragon House, 1998). She's the former poetry editor of *The Nation*, received five Pushcart Prizes and the Frost Medal from the Poetry Society of America, and is a Distinguished Professor of English at Baruch College.

1. **Apprentice Yourself to a Master:** Find a poet you can't live without, who has changed your life. Read everything by that poet: poetry collections, essays, letters if available, biographies.
2. **Read Your Poems Aloud, to Yourself and to Others:** You can also hear poets read their work on Poetry Foundation's website and in some cases, on YouTube.
3. **Swap Poems with a Small Group of Poets for Criticism:** This is why taking classes can be so helpful.
4. **Work Hard:** Make writing a full-time occupation.
5. **Be Ruthless When It Comes to Interruptions:** Hang a sign over your desk that says NO DISTRACTIONS.
6. **Go to Readings and Buy Books:** Find out what other poets are doing and what people are reading.
7. **Don't Try to Publish if It Doesn't Come Easy:** Early publication means zilch to a poet's development. As Emily Dickinson wrote, "Publication- is the Auction/Of the Mind of Man . . . /But reduce no Human Spirit/To Disgrace of Price."

CHAPTER 6

Anthologizing

HOW *NOT* TO ANTHOLOGIZE

1. **Collect Only Your Own Work:** Put together everything you've written but never published over two decades, sending it to an editor with the title "An Anthology Of Me."

2. **Gather Your Favorite Poetry, Fiction, Essays and Plays by Others:** The theme could be "The Best Writing Ever," crossing all genres to be inclusionary. Don't bother to research The Best American Essays, Best American Poetry or Best American Short Stories series that started in 1915.

3. **Put Together *New Yorker* Short Stories You Loved:** Don't check to see if the magazine owns and anthologizes its own work. (Hint: it does.)

4. **Pick a Topic that's Been Done—Like Barbie or Baseball:** So what if there's already a bunch of collections out there? That shows there's a big audience for it. Good time for an update.

5. **In Your Proposal, List Famous Writers Who'll Contribute Without Asking First:** Don't bother checking with anyone. Once you get a book deal, they'll come around.

6. **Assume Contributors Won't Need Payment:** You'll need the advance to cover your own bills. Writers should be honored to be included in your book.

7. **Rewrite All the Work:** When someone hands in a piece you don't love, kick it into shape and send it back to them saying, "Let's use my version, which is much better."
8. **Pay Each Writer Differently:** Don't worry that they might know each other and compare notes.
9. **Include Only Published Work:** Assume when publishers say they want original material they're not being literal. Copy the way Roxane Gay did it, forgetting that she's a bestselling, award-winning writer and editor who publishers seek out.
10. **Forget Platform, Connections and Experience:** How hard could it be to get a bunch of writers to contribute new material? You don't need a book out or a PhD for that.

BETTER WAYS TO LAUNCH AN ANTHOLOGY

I love anthologies, which I've always seen as the Greatest Hits albums for literature. In college, I schlepped around the fat *Norton Anthology of Poetry* with verse by everyone from Geoffrey Chaucer and Emily Dickinson to Nikki Giovanni. Later, teaching college courses, I recommended my students get Phillip Lopate's magnificent *Art of the Personal Essay: An Anthology from the Classical Era to the Present,* where I devoured everyone from Virginia Woolf to James Baldwin to Adrienne Rich. After merging lives and bookshelves with my husband, I noticed our shelves became crowded with the testosterone-filled *Prentice Hall Anthology of Science Fiction and Fantasy* of Tolkien, Bram Stoker and Stephen King, along with David Halberstam's *Best American Sports Writing of the Century's* Red Smith and A. J. Liebling. At bookstores I saw tons of compilations of literary work by multiple authors in one volume. I assumed they were done in-house and restricted to famous scribes and editors. I had no idea that anybody could sell an anthology by pitching it with a short proposal. I'd never considered doing one myself.

Then my agent sold Cathi Hanauer's *The Bitch in the House: 26 Women Tell the Truth About Sex, Solitude, Work, Motherhood, and Marriage.* I loved the provocative personal takes on the battle of the sexes by Pam Houston, Vivian Gornick, Hope Edelman and Chitra Divakaruni. The book was such a hit in 2003 that Hanauer's husband Daniel Jones launched *The Bastard on the Couch: 27 Men Try Really Hard to Explain Their Feelings About Love, Loss, Fatherhood, and Freedom,* which the same publisher put out a year later. After editing pieces about sex, commitment and the male biological clock, Jones decided he liked editing. A *New York Times* style section editor saw how popular these relationship essays were and offered them the weekly Modern Love column that Jones and Hanauer began together. They decided it was a one-person job. Not wanting to ruin a great marriage over a love column, Jones took it over and wound up editing several *Modern Love* collections of his own.

I asked Hanauer how she'd launched such a wildly successful anthology. It's always important to see what kind of books are already out there in your genre and indeed she'd been inspired by *Here Lies My Heart: Essays on Why We Marry, Why We Don't, and What We Find There* and *Mothers Who Think: Tales of Real Life Parenthood* by *Salon* editors Camille Peri and Kate Moses. "I was a working mother with two young kids and I felt, as did many of my friends, that we were still doing everything domestic," Hanauer said. "We had walked through the doors feminism opened for us—the ability to have a marriage and children and a career/income on a level with men—only to find that, once the children arrived, we needed a wife. Things did not feel fair. I was a writer and an editor, as were many of my friends and colleagues. So I decided to do a book of essays where we contributed our own version of the dilemma that was making us so angry."

Hanauer had already published a novel, but was too busy to finish more long fiction. Because she had a literary agent and a book editor, she sold *Bitch in the House* with the provocative title, a 12-page proposal and an intro explaining her concept. Doing an anthology required more editing than writing, which appealed to the harried mother. Perhaps most importantly, she secured commitments from well-known authors she knew from her days as a women's magazine editor. She paid each writer $500 from her advance for pieces between 2,000 and 4,000 words. It did so well that Hanauer published a follow-up anthology in 2017 called *The Bitch Is Back: Older, Wiser, and (Getting) Happier.*

The worst part, Hanauer said, was writers who committed but couldn't come through, missed the deadline, refused to be edited or acted like divas. The best perk was that the book became a phenomenon—the right idea at the right time that "caught the zeitgeist." She confessed she loved "working with a bunch of incredible writers you admire to create something beautiful and profound and watching the book come together. A group project is nice for a writer whose work is usually solitary. I met lifelong friends. It was a thrilling, if sometimes stressful experience."

Wanting a thrilling, stressful experience myself, I considered pitching an anthology too. Tired of trying to fix a messy novel that wasn't coming together, I found it much easier to edit 200 to 300 pages of other people's work than finish my own. But I couldn't think of a great topic.

I'd spent a dozen years co-teaching a special charity writing workshop at a soup kitchen in Manhattan with the *New Yorker* icon Ian Frazier. The participants were homeless, in addiction recovery, ex-cons and people down on their luck who needed a free meal. We'd give them free pens and notebooks and offer prompts like "My Best Mistake," "So I Lied," "The Worst Day" and "When One Door Closes, Another Opens." After writing on our suggested subjects for an hour, they'd read their work out loud. Their stories were so powerful that I thought: this should be a book. When a former student's husband became an editor at a small Christian publisher, I gave her a copy of recent pieces from the workshop we had typed and said, "He should publish this anthology." He did!

They offered a $5,000 advance for *Food for the Soul: Selections from the Holy Apostles Soup Kitchen Writer's Workshop.* After I read Marlo Thomas's anthology *The Right Words at the Right Time*, with proceeds going to St. Jude's Research Hospital, I also wanted to help a good cause. I'd sold other books for larger advances, as had Frazier. So we split the money between the twenty-five writers who really needed it, giving each $200 and copies of the book. All the royalties went back to the soup kitchen. It was in the *New York Times*, on NPR and *The Today Show*. *Publishers Weekly* called it "funny, gritty and brutally honest—writing that attests to a raw spirituality formed and informed by life on the streets." The book was a huge success—except for the money part, since I put in a thousand hours and made nothing.

While charity books bring good karma, most authors and editors want anthologies to be financially viable too. I was thrilled the next year when my colleague Ruth Andrew Ellenson asked me to contribute to her book *The Modern Jewish Girl's Guide to Guilt*. Though she hadn't published a book before, Ellenson sold it to Dutton for enough to pay twenty-eight contributors $500 each for essays. Mine, on quitting guilt, was 3,500 words. All the writers did a bunch of fun events. It was a bestseller and won a Jewish Book Award. Since then I've been in dozens of anthologies, paid anywhere from nothing to $2,500 for a piece. If it's a topic I liked I often said yes for the exposure and community.

Few anthologies sell as well as *The Bitch in the House* and *The Modern Jewish Girl's Guide to Guilt*. Yet Sari Botton, a former student who is now the editor at Catapult, had two hits. After she couldn't afford New York City, she moved upstate, ambivalent about leaving.

"Everywhere I went in my new life upstate, I met people talking about the same thing I was talking about: leaving New York City, and having very mixed feelings about it," she told me. "So if there's something everyone around you is talking about, and you feel passionate about the topic, it's a sign you're onto something worth exploring from a variety of angles and voices."

Researching her topic, Botton found similar books—but they were dated, out of print and not as sharply focused as hers. She wrote a 2-page proposal, including the list of twenty-eight writers who'd offer new material, many whom she knew from her editorial work, big hitters like

Cheryl Strayed and Roxane Gay. Botton was offered a $7,000 advance from the indie female publisher Seal Press for *Goodbye to All That: Writers on Loving and Leaving New York*. It did so well that Botton made more from Simon and Schuster for the sequel *Never Can Say Goodbye: Writers on Their Unshakeable Love for New York,* which came out in paperback in 2014. It was also a bestseller that still earns her royalties.

Botton's Seal Press editor Laura Mazer said *Goodbye to All That* and Lilly Dancyger's 2018 anthology *Burn It Down: Women Writing about Anger* were the strongest sellers she'd bought over her long career. She admitted that typically the advances for anthologies are lower because sales projections are usually smaller than for single-author titles. Plus the anthology editor who receives the advance has to pay the contributors. According to Mazer (now a literary agent), the biggest mistake authors make is not having fresh enough ideas and not getting well-known writers to commit to a project. From the standpoint of an agent and editor considering anthologies, the most important factors are:

1. A strong clear concept that immediately resonates with readers
2. Having well-known contributors—bestselling authors, celebrities and other boldface names
3. Great writing

Speaking of great writing, a piece Botton published when she was an editor at *Longreads* led to its own anthology. Michele Filgate's poignant essay *Lacuna* chronicles her sexual abuse by her stepfather, a man her mother stayed married to. In 2017's #MeToo environment, Filgate's essay went viral with Botton's new suggested title *What My Mother and I Don't Talk About*. A 3-page proposal along with her essay led Simon and Schuster to snatch it up for a debut hardcover anthology with that same name. As a book reviewer, former bookseller and fellow National Book Critics Circle board member, Filgate easily found fifteen well-known writers to contribute, including Cathi Hanauer and

Sari Botton (yes, half of publishing knows one another), along with male authors Alexander Chee, Brandon Taylor and André Acimen.

Botton's idea to call it *What My Mother and I Don't Talk About* underscored the importance of an eye-catching title.

"I think having a compelling topic is the most crucial step for selling an anthology," Filgate said via email. After her essay came out, "so many people told me they had their own stories about what they wouldn't talk about with their mother. It became obvious almost immediately that this was a great topic for a book," she added. It helped that she already had a platform on social media and knew writers from The National Book Critics Circle and hosting events at indie bookstores. Her proposal included a list of writers who committed to the project, as well as a list of fantasy contributors. Like Mazer, she advises those who want to sell an anthology to have a list of well-known writers attached to the proposal. "You need to have recognizable names so their fans will buy the book."

Simon and Schuster also published the 2017 acclaimed fiction collection *Everyday People: The Color—of Life—a Short Story Anthology* with Jason Reynolds, Brandon Taylor and Alexander Chee (yes, the same writers do a lot of anthologies). It was edited by Jennifer Baker, an acclaimed editor who inherited the project from the late Brook Stephenson, who wanted to see a collection celebrating people of color. Perhaps being well connected, as a literary agent, helped Andrew Blauner launch several idiosyncratic anthologies including *The Peanut Papers: Writers and Cartoonists on Charlie Brown, Snoopy and the Gang, and the Meaning of Life* (Library of America, 2019), *In Their Lives: Great Writers on Great Beatles Songs* (Penguin, 2017) and *The Good Book: Writers Reflect on Favorite Bible Passages* (Simon and Schuster, 2017).

While Houghton Mifflin is famous for their *Best American Short Story, Essay* and *Humor* books, Cleis Press in New Jersey has published many LGBTQ-themed anthologies like *Best Gay Erotica of the Year*, *Urban Lesbian Erotica* and *Twice the Pleasure: Bisexual Woman's Erotica* edited by Rachel Kramer Bussel, my fellow NYU grad who specializes in erotic lit. Beacon Press in Boston is known for putting out anthologies with diverse voices not often heard in mainstream publishing, such as *Kori: The Beacon Anthology of Korean American Fiction; American Muslim Men on Love, Sex and Intimacy; Making Waves: An Anthology of Writings By and about Asian American Women;* and *Age Ain't Nothing But a Number: Black Women Explore Midlife. Bullets into Bells: Poets and Citizens Respond to Gun Violence* has a foreword by gun-control advocate Gabrielle Giffords, another smart way to package your project.

To get a sense of the wide range of topics you can pick for an anthology, here are some I've contributed pieces for: *The New York Times Book Review 2000. The Barbie Chronicles. Madonna and Me. Beyond the Bedroom Door. The Best American Humor. Wedding Cake for Breakfast: Essays on the Unforgettable First Year of Marriage. My Body, My Words. How Does That Make You Feel: True Confessions from Both Sides of the Therapy Couch. Fury: Women's Lived Experiences during the Trump Era.*

THE DOWNSIDE OF DOING AN ANTHOLOGY

1. It's hard to get famous people to commit. Unless you work in publishing, a Hollywood movie company, bookstores or PR, you might have to waste a lot of hours figuring how to ace this type of literary networking.

2. There's a lot of organizing, scheduling, emailing, proofreading and copyediting you will be in charge of before the more glamorous book events start. Botton admitted it can be "a bit of an administrative nightmare."

3. Advances are small. While many students I know earned $50,000 to $100,000 for debut novels, memoirs or self-help books from major publishers, the average first anthology advance I've heard of is closer to $10,000.

4. You have to pay contributors yourself. Even if you offer just $100 a piece, with twenty contributors that adds up to $2,000 out of your pocket (minus taxes and the literary agency's 15 percent).

5. Many writers are notoriously flaky and depressed. I heard of one famous scribe who cancelled a piece they promised because writing it made them sad. Some contributors could disappear and not hand in their piece at all. Or refuse to be edited or change their mind last-minute. You may have to be part shrink, agent, editor, friend, collaborator and nursemaid.

6. It's hard to get press. A first novel, memoir or biography is a bigger deal to literary gatekeepers. An anthology, not so much. They are reviewed and profiled less, especially coming from small houses.

7. You may be usurped. While the editor does most of the work and their name is on the book and reviews, celebrity contributors can get the glory and press mentions. They sometimes get big payments for selling their piece to be excerpted in a top newspaper or magazine, causing you—the book's creator—to lament, "What am I, chopped liver?"

BENEFITS OF DOING AN ANTHOLOGY

1. You get to spend more time editing than writing. The author who earns the advance sometimes only needs to pen a short book proposal or an intro and sometimes not even that. You can be younger or older, less experienced in publishing or battling writer's block that keeps you from finishing your novel—as long as you have a winning concept, title and can convince luminaries to contribute.

2. It's a shortcut to being a published author. Instead of spending five years struggling to craft the Great American Novel, you can spend five weeks (or less) coming up with a stellar concept in a short proposal.

3. It's collaborative. If you're lonely working by yourself at home, this kind of project can provide community. I've done many fun group readings for the projects I've been part of, making friends and connections along the way.

4.	You meet elder statesmen. To do an anthology, you often need star writers. You can approach anyone you admire to ask them to work with you. If you can't figure out how to get emails or phone numbers, go through their publisher, manager or agent. I was thrilled my mentor Ian Frazier co-edited *Food for the Soul* and wrote the foreword. Plus I got to read with Meg Wolitzer, Erica Jong, Molly Jong-Fast and Daphne Merkin at other anthology events.

5.	You can push your own agenda. Proceeds can go to a cause you believe in or you can choose a topic you feel strongly about. It can be anything from sexual harassment to racism to your brand of politics, as in *Conservatism: An Anthology of Social and Political Thought from David Hume to the Present; Thirty Ways of Looking at Hillary: Reflections by Women Writers;* and *The Dangerous Case of Donald Trump: 27 Psychiatrists and Mental Health Experts Assess a President.*

6.	It can accelerate your career. If you are good at organizing and editing, you can become well known, on TV, radio and an award-winning writer or bestseller after penning as few as 5 pages.

7.	Any topic in the world can fly—though British Goblins, Food Poetry, Dental Humor and The Big Book of Lesbian Horse Stories are already taken.

EXPERT ADVICE ON ANTHOLOGIES

I asked my former editor Laura Mazer for advice about selling an anthology.

She should know. For a decade and a half, as an executive editor at Seal Press, Basic Books and Counterpoint Press, Mazer became a maven on anthologizing. She bought *Without a Net: The Female Experience of Growing Up Working Class* (2004) by Michelle Tea, Sari Botton's bestseller *Goodbye to All That: Writers on Loving and Leaving New York* (2013), Sherry Amatenstein's *How Does That Make You Feel: True Confessions from Both Sides of the Therapy Couch* (2016), Lilly Dancyger's *Burn It Down: Women Writing about Anger* (2018) and Lizzie Skurnick's

Pretty Bitches: On Being Called Crazy, Angry, Bossy, Frumpy, Feisty, and All the Other Words That Are Used to Undermine Woman (2020). Mazer is now a literary agent at Wendy Sherman Associations where she hopes to sell anthologies. Here's her take on how.

1. **What's It About?** Having a clear, bold concept is essential, so choose a provocative title and focus on a hot-button issue or a topic that's highly relatable. The title and subtitle should be immediately "gettable." (I quickly understood the concept and said yes when asked to contribute to the books *Modern Jewish Girl's Guide to Guilt; Madonna and Me: Women Writers on the Queen of Pop;* and *Fast Funny Women: 75 Essays of Flash Nonfiction.*)

2. **Who Do You Know?** Big names sell anthologies: think of famous people in your field you can ask to contribute. Consider old professors, bosses or luminaries you admire and might have some connection to. Pro tip: if someone says no to writing an essay, don't just walk away. Try asking if they'll consider giving you an endorsement later instead.

3. **Who Committed?** Write a proposal (see chapter on nonfiction proposals) with your great title and subtitle, your full bio and an explanation of how you'll market and promote it. You'll also need a contributors list and comparable titles. Include at least one terrific essay as a sample of the content, and top the whole thing off with an overview arguing why your concept is urgent and why readers will be eager to buy it.

4. **Who Sells Anthologies?** Research literary agents. Check agency websites and credits to see if they handle this type of book. If not, read the acknowledgments pages of anthologies you admire to see who represented it and also note who put it out. If you can't find an agent, research smaller publishers who do anthologies where un-agented authors can submit directly. (For unusual or niche ideas, like my religious book *Food for the Soul,* research specialty presses.)

5. **Why You?** Play up why you're the perfect person to steer this book. The author of *The Modern Girl's Guide to Guilt* mentioned she was born in Jerusalem and had two parents who were rabbis. *Wanderlust: A Modern Yogi's Guide to Finding Your Best Self* co-editor Sarah Herrington was a longtime yoga teacher. You don't need sophisticated expertise in your subject. Laura Barcella, editor of *Madonna and Me*, emphasized she'd been a Madonna devotee since age six.

6. **Who Are Your Readers?** Build buzz for the project by establishing your platform before the book is submitted. Ways to do this? Have significant followings on social media and/or publish essays on the topic and/or appear on TV or the radio or podcasts talking about your issue and/or have a big job in a related field.

7. **Get In the Door:** Be in other anthologies. There are "calls for pieces" in *Poets and Writers* and *Writer's Digest* Magazines, and also in social media groups for writers. Being part of an anthology will teach you a lot about how they work—and connect you with other good writers who may want to participate in your project.

CHAPTER 7

Humor and Graphics

HOW TO BE HUMORLESS

1. **Type Up Your Favorite Jokes and Send Them to an Editor:** Make sure you send a note saying, "You should publish this."
2. **Mix Up Genres:** Write a novel or memoir that happens to be amusing and call it a "humor book" when submitting to agents and book editors to keep everyone on their toes.
3. **Submit Your Humor Manuscript Everywhere:** Who needs an agent or an editor? Email it to *SNL, Comedy Central* and *Jimmy Fallon* even though they make it clear that all submissions need to be in a specific format that is not book-form.
4. **Gather Material You've Heard Elsewhere:** Don't keep track of whose jokes and comedy routines you're stealing. Once it's out there in the zeitgeist it's in the public domain, right?
5. **Confuse Stand-Up Comedy with Sit-Down Humor:** Send a reel of your comedy club act to literary agents and book editors without bothering to put any of it down on the page.
6. **Send Out Funny YouTube and TikTok Links:** If a literary agent likes it, they can just send it to book editors as is.
7. **Add Recommendations from Family and Friends:** If an agent or editor gives you criticism, let them know they're wrong since "this killed over Thanksgiving dinner."

8. **Avoid Getting Clips:** *McSweeney's, The New Yorker Shouts & Murmurs, Weekly Humorist, Funny Times* and other humor magazines don't pay that much. You need to start with big bucks for a book.

9. **Follow the Stars:** Emulate humorous books by Amy Schumer, Trevor Noah, Jon Stewart, Samantha Bee and Jenny McCarthy, putting yourself in the same category as famous people who have television shows. And don't take the time to note which were sold as essay collections or memoirs. Funny is funny, am I right guys?

10. **Post It all on Tumblr, Facebook, Insta and Medium:** That way everybody can see how hilarious you are. And editors and agents love selling work that you've already given away for free.

EXPERT ADVICE ON HUMOR

While an editor's response to any kind of writing is a matter of personal taste, humor is particularly subjective. While you want to trust your sense of absurdity and hilarity, packaging and publishing it requires more finesse than funniness. That's why I asked the advice of long-time editor at Random House and Workman Publishing Company, my buddy Bruce Tracy, who has edited many hilarious books by such humorists as Merrill Markoe, Alan Zweibel, Dan Zevin, Carol Leifer, Firoozeh Dumas and Laurie Notaro. Four of those books were Thurber Prize for American Humor finalists, one won and many were best-sellers. Humor books are still popular and can garner anywhere from $5,000 advances from a mainstream publisher to six figures, depending on everything from your background to how much your off-beat sensibility translates to mainstream. Here's his suggestions for standing out in the jam-packed comedy category.

1. **Get Clear on Your Genre:** Some fictional fun-fests are considered narrative comic novels, like Zweibel's *The Other Schulman*. Others are humorous memoirs, like Dumas's *Funny in Farsi*. Notaro's *The Idiot Girl* and *The Flaming Tantrum of Death* and many hit volumes by David Sedaris are called essay collections. These books

are pitched to agents and editors who handle memoirs, novels and essays. They are different from the impulse buy, gag gift and novelty-type humor books sold near cash registers at Urban Outfitter-type retailers, like the old tongue-in-cheek reference guide *The Preppy Handbook* and its sequel *True Prep,* and *All My Friends Are Dead.* Almost all major houses publish impulse–buy humor to some degree. Those particularly strong in this arena are Quirk, Chronicle, Sourcebooks, Andrews McMeel and such imprints as Three Rivers Press.

2. **Study Parodies and Satire:** A popular humor subgenre is parody, which takes off on something already out there, like the infamous *Is Martha Stewart Living?*; *Women Who Run With Poodles; The Bitches of Madison County; Goodnight iPad;* or *The Dangerous Book for Dogs.* The trick with these is to come up with a provocative title that illuminates the content, and hasn't been done before. If it's parody, clearly label it as such on the cover so you don't get sued. Many publishers and booksellers are weary of the proliferation of titles with obscenities: *The Life-Changing Magic of Not Giving a F*ck. Fuck Off Coronavirus, I'm Coloring. I Used to Be a Miserable F*ck. Unfu*ck Yourself. The Zen as F*uck Journals. No Fucks Given Guides. Everything Is F*ucked* and my L.A. friend Amy Alkon's *Good Manners for Nice People Who Sometimes Say F*ck* and *Unf*ckology.* By the time you jump on a book trend, it's usually over. So we may actually be all fucked out by now. (I sometimes prefer witty and provocative to profane; my all-time favorite humor book titles are Cynthia Heimel's *If You Can't Live Without Me, Why Aren't You Dead Yet?* and *Get Your Tongue Out of My Mouth, I'm Kissing You Goodbye.*)

3. **Sell Short Witty Pieces:** Read, subscribe and submit work to *McSweeney's, The New Yorker* Shouts & Murmurs, *The Onion, Weekly Humorist, Cracked*.com, *Madmagazine.com* and *Funny Times.* "There's the old saying, 'To get published, it helps to get published,'" Tracy said. Indeed, after my former student Fiona

Taylor's sharp satires landed in the *New Yorker's* Daily Shouts and McSweeney's, she sold her humorous book *New Erotica for Feminists: Satirical Fantasies: Sexual Fantasies of Love, Lust and Equal Pay*, written with fellow editors of the satiric feminist website theBelladonna.comedy.com, which offers other satirists and comedians an audience for their comedy.

4. **The Internet Is Your Oyster:** Most modern humor gets tried out on the web for free, whether it's tweeted like *Sh*t My Dad Says*, newer comics like @DuchessGoldblatt, Sophia Fraioli and Lauren Kaelin's Tumblr blog *When Parents Text*, or Issa Rae's YouTube web series *Awkward Black Girl*, which became a book and an award-winning HBO sitcom *Insecure*. Even if you hate social media, it's a great, easy, fast and free testing ground to see if your snark or quirkiness can find an audience other than the beer buddies who think you're a riot.

5. **Propose a Humor Book:** While most comic novels require the entire manuscript, a short proposal will suffice for impulse-buy books. *The 776 Stupidest Things Ever Said*, by Ross and Kathryn Petras, which Tracy published in the pre-internet days, was sold on 20 pages of sample material. It was a bestseller, spawning fifteen spinoff titles (with a total of 6 million in print) as well as a Stupidest calendar that sold over 4.6 million copies. Though humor pitches can still be short, if your book is based on work originally posted online, you'll need some original material that hasn't all been given away for free. And, of course, a platform always helps. (After I'd published relationship humor in *Cosmopolitan*, I was asked to write my humor book, *The Male to Female Dictionary*, by Berkley Press, for their series with Comedy Central.)

6. **Other Media Matters:** Whether it's stand-up, a one-man or one-woman show, radio, podcasts, TV sitcoms or film comedies, there's a huge crossover, and authors coming in with their own audience always interest editors. Sarah Cooper—who blew up with her Trump lip-synching—has 330,000 YouTube subscribers, two

humor books *100 Tricks to Appear Smart in Meetings* (2016) and *How to Be Successful Without Hurting Men's Feelings* (2018), and a Netflix special. Going viral is a very good step towards book publication.

7. **Think of Your Book as a Gift:** Ask yourself: Who would I give this to? And why? *Toddlers Are A**holes: It's Not Your Fault* (2015) by Bunmi Laditan, a Montreal mom who wrote for Parenting.com and Mothering.com, was pitched to stressed-out parents who need a laugh. Tom Friedman's *1,000 Unforgettable Senior Moments: Of Which We Could Remember Only 254* (2017) was geared towards older readers with funny bones. Cartoonist Mo Welch wrote and illustrated her book *How to Die Alone: The Foolproof Guide to Not Helping Yourself* (2019), aimed at singles with a sense of humor. If you don't know who your book is for, figure it out first.

EXPERT ADVICE FROM A GRAPHIC BOOK AUTHOR

I knew there were different kinds of book-length work combining words with sequential art. There was Manga (the Japanese word for "comic") superhero stories and non-superhero stories, as well as personal narratives called Perzines. Yet I had no idea how one would start a graphic book. So I emailed Ben Katchor. The first cartoonist to receive a MacArthur Fellowship, he's author of eleven books of picture stories I love like *Julius Knipl, Real Estate Photographer* (1996) and *The Jew of New York* (1999). Katchor is the subject of the documentary *Pleasures of Urban Decay* and a lively *New Yorker* profile; Pulitzer Prize–winning novelist Michael Chabon called him "the creator of the last great American comic strip."

I told Katchor that I was a huge fan of his who bought five copies of his latest, *The Diary Restaurant* (2020), for my mother and her friends who grew up on the Lower East Side. (Always lead with the multiple copies of an author's book you just bought.) I was psyched that he offered advice to aspiring cartoonists and artists who want to be authors too. Here are his suggestions.

1. **Read Graphic Art in Many Forms:** Katchor loved comics as a kid, making his own. He published fanzines in his teens. His work starts as a contemplation of an experience, he said, but spans several genres. *The Jew of New York* is historical fiction. *Knipl,* based on his comic strip, is fictional but modern while *The Diary Restaurant* combines history with graphic memoir. Being up on what's out there will show how to push the boundaries yourself.

2. **Get Schooled:** In college in the 1970s, it was difficult to study text-image combinations outside of theatre or film, Katchor recalled. So he alternated between learning literature and painting while continuing to make comics. The idea of purified forms of text or image-making didn't appeal to him. He's now an associate professor in the Illustration program at Parson's The New School, where students study experimental comics, animation and graphic narrative. He runs their New York Comics and Picture-story Symposium, a free online lecture series about text-images. He's also given talks at colleges and museums accompanied by slide projections of his work.

3. **Study Different Subjects:** Katchor recommends you take all kinds of classes and immerse yourself in world culture. His eclectic passions have been fodder for his comic strips exploring history, architecture, Jewish culture and urban design, as well as musical-theatre shows with Mark Mulcahy.

4. **Explore Your Field:** Check out the many wonderful alternative comics festivals all over the world. While I've had students who swear by the annual Comic Cons across the country, Katchor also recommends Comic Arts Brooklyn and the MoCCA festival. You'll see what's happening in the graphic arts universe, stay up-to-date, meet your people and become better versed in the different arenas where you can work in the future.

5. **Develop Cohorts, Colleagues and Mentors:** Some cartoonists used to break into the field by working as an apprentice to an established cartoonist or interning in the cartoon or art departments of *The New Yorker, Mad* or *Cracked Magazine, National Lampoon* or *Village Voice*. As comics moved from commercial art and journalism to a form of graphic literature, apprenticeships and publishing jobs became less viable, Katchor explained. Aside from taking classes, another option these days is peer-to-peer learning through online groups such as The American Library Association Graphic Novel and Comics Round Table on Facebook, Instagram and Twitter.

6. **Get Comic Clips:** Katchor published his work in *The Kingsman*, the student newspaper of Brooklyn College where he went to school. Most cartoonists build an audience through self-publishing and promotion. Now that's happening online, through webcomic sites like Reddit, Tumblr, Imgur, Webtoons, Tapas, Hiveworks, MemeCenter, HUGELOL and digital platforms like Gumroad and Comixology. Though you probably won't make money right away and may have to spend it, it's a good start to get a platform.

7. **Try Selling Your Work:** Getting clips to show off will help you become a paid contributor. Katchor contributing regularly to *Raw,* an avant-garde comics magazine that *Maus* author Art Spiegelman and his wife Francoise Mouly put out. They recommended him to *New York Press,* where he freelanced before breaking into *Slate* and *The New Yorker.* Katchor recommends perfecting a short-form comic strip before trying novel-length. Most of his books are compilations of short strips, not comics conceived as book-length projects. Try every venue, online and in print, to see if you can find somewhere that might be attuned to the sort of work you make. Don't give up on your passion—Katchor was repeatedly told there was no market for what he was doing—until he created the one he keeps winning prizes for.

SECTION 3:
FICTIONALIZING

CHAPTER 8

Adult Fiction

HOW *NOT* TO BE A PUBLISHED NOVELIST

1. **Shun All Fiction:** That way you'll be original and not influenced by other work.
2. **Avoid Literature and Writing Classes**: You don't have the time or the money, you just want the big bucks from Simon and Schuster quickly.
3. **Finish 100 Pages in Two Weeks:** Hey, getting it all down is easy, so keep kicking out 20 or 20 pages a day.
4. **Forget to Revise:** You don't want your pages to lose their fresh, immediate quality.
5. **Find Famous Novelists to Help You Get Published:** Stalk them on social media with a link to your partial manuscript, offering a percentage when your book goes big.
6. **Query Agents Right Away:** Google literary agencies and email the first half of your book to any names that pop up, mentioning that you've never published anything, don't read fiction and work in a different field.
7. **Ignore Guidelines on the Agency's Website:** You don't have time. So what if the agent doesn't handle any genre fiction or poetry and you're submitting sci-fi prose poetry in iambic pentameter? Your work is so dazzling, you'll be the exception.

8. **Pitch a Series Before Selling One Book:** Tell them you have many books in you, like that *Game of Thrones* author.

9. **Send It to TV/Film Producers Too**: Let them know yours will be way better than *The Hunger Games* when you finish, though you'll need them to float you an advance now, so you can quit your day job to focus on your writing.

10. **Self-Publish with No Research:** Never mind all the authors, agents, editors or producers who ignored you, without figuring out why your work was rejected. Hey, you could become a millionaire like the woman who wrote *Fifty Shades of Grey*. Mainstream publishers are all elitists not interested in great fiction by real people anyway.

BETTER WAYS TO GO

If your goal is to publish a novel, the best way to start is: write a novel. While this popular genre is defined as an invented prose narrative of book length about imaginary characters and made-up events, many authors (like me) have published autobiographical novels inspired by events that really happened. It's a tradition employed by Ernest Hemingway's *The Sun Also Rises,* Zora Neale Hurston's *Their Eyes Were Watching God,* Amy Tan's *The Joy Luck Club* and Kate Elizabeth Russell's more recent debut *My Dark Vanessa*. Yet the form is different from memoirs, journalism or true-life chronicles, as novels are considered fictitious and unreal, although (confusingly) they can be hyper-realistic.

If it's your debut or your other published books didn't soar to best-sellerdom (me again!), you probably won't sell a novel with a proposal, treatment, summary or a few chapters, or even half the book, the way nonfiction can often be sold. You'll have to finish the whole shebang. Publishing three novels and reviewing thousands over the years, I've found the average fictional project from mainstream publishers is 230 pages double-spaced (how technophobes like me calculate length) or about 60,000 words (how the rest of the world counts).

Despite the National Novel Writing Month contests, it won't help you to see this as a quick, light undertaking, especially if you're serious about finding an agent and top publisher to pay you an advance. (Self-publishing is a different category altogether.) Think: one year to complete a sellable first draft if you're wildly lucky. Five years average. It could be two decades if, like Marilynne Robinson, you're aiming for a literary masterpiece like *Housekeeping*. I'll never forget her speech at the National Book Critics Circle award, where she said two words ("Twenty Years") and received a standing ovation. I guessed that many literati in the audience also had long-simmering projects requiring perseverance. My own first (comic, non-award-winning) novel took thirteen years from start to publication.

If you're impatient and scared off by that duration, skip to the chapters on how-to's, anthologies, essay collections, humor or cookbooks—which can gel (and sell) much faster. Or consider genre fiction, which many authors can craft and publish in under twelve months. However, beware: if you ask twenty different novelists how they did it, they'll share twenty different strategies, each swearing by their method alone. Here are the suggestions that helped me conquer this most prestigious of book categories.

1. **Read What You Want to Write:** If you're not familiar with fiction currently being published, chances are you won't write it well. You'll be working in a vacuum with no context. (Picture someone saying "I want to be a doctor" without ever visiting one or studying medicine.) While it's better for an aspiring author to read all kinds of books, before you begin I'd advise you to study at least twenty bestselling, award-winning specimens of the exact kind you aspire to. (Google: "Bestselling award-winning novels" with your subgenre.) Consider this your homework and prerequisite research, to see what's already out there, what's possible and what you might be able to add to the field. I've never read a good novel by someone who didn't read them. When an aspiring student novelist once told

me "I'm not really into reading books," I guessed he'd never publish one. (So far, he hasn't.)

2. **Figure Out Which Subset Your Project Falls Under:** There are many kinds of novels to pick: Adult, Young Adult, New Adult (how many kinds of adults are there?), not to mention Middle-Grade, Historical, Romance, Comic, Mystery, Thriller, Science Fiction, Western, Horror, Literary, Commercial and many in between. An adult literary novel is probably the most difficult to craft and sell, and genre fiction may be the easiest, depending on such factors as your age, talent, platform, background and obsessions. Pay attention to correct category names so you don't mistakenly tell an agent you are writing "a sci-fi nonfiction mystery thriller" or "a fictional novel." In which section will your book be shelved? If you don't know yet, go to a bookstore to explore. While you're there, buy a bunch of books to support the profession, so it still exists by the time you finish.

3. **Take a Fiction- or Novel-Writing Class:** In decades of studying and teaching writing, I never met anyone who sat alone at home, finished a book of fiction they submitted and received a call saying, "We love it and will send you a lot of money." I have, however, seen many writing students workshop novels they later sold. I've even hosted a bunch of their book parties. It's hard to make a living as a writer, so many authors also teach. Check websites of schools and writing programs and pay attention to the bios of professors. There may be special classes for each genre. The New School, where I teach, has an entire program dedicated to children's literature run by David Levithan, a luminary editor in that arena.

If you have a choice, study with someone whose work you admire and want to emulate. If you can't take their class, at least buy and read their books. *New York Times* bestselling novelist Caroline Leavitt, author of ten books including *Pictures of You* and *Cruel Beautiful World*, shared a karmic principle her mentor taught her: "The late great Carolyn See told me every week, I should write a charming note to an author I admire. Don't ask for anything. Just thank them," Leavitt said. "Tell them what their work meant to you. That builds community and makes you—and the author—feel good."

4. **Scrawl Notes:** If you can't take a class that will give you assignments, start writing on your own. When I'm contemplating a novel, I get an empty notebook and jot down all my ideas for the complicated, crazy story I plan to tell. I write a list of potential characters, scenes, chapters, actions and twists. I like to conjure up a hero, their goal and the obstacles that keep my protagonist from getting what they want. (Check out the "Hero's Journey" concept, coined by Joseph Campbell, who George Lucas credited with influencing the *Star Wars* saga.) Sometimes I have sentences in my mind I capture on paper. Many successful writers chart out their whole plot in a complex outline. There are others who swear all you need to begin is the first line. I know Luddites who write the entire first draft on lined paper or speak it into a tape recorder. Certain old-timers still use a typewriter, though these days the majority of novelists start and end on a computer. (Upside: you can easily keep all of your drafts.) If you follow my rule that "You can do anything as long as it works," you'll know what works better after you study top examples in the genre.

5. **Come Up with an Evocative Working Title:** On my bookshelves are novels whose names intrigued me immediately from Flannery O'Connor's *A Good Man Is Hard to Find,* Michael Chabon's *The Amazing Adventures of Kavalier and Clay, The Brief Wondrous Life of Oscar Wao* by Junot Diaz, Milan Kundera's *The Unbearable Lightness of Being* and Jennifer Egan's *A Visit from the Goon Squad.* If you can't come up with anything juicy or profound, borrow a phrase from the Bible, like John Steinbeck's *East of Eden,* Edith Wharton's *House of Mirth* and Toni Morrison's *Song of Solomon.* Don't worry if it's not perfect; you can always change it. But be aware that your agent, editor or publisher might change it for you. That's often for

the good, since Harper Lee's *To Kill a Mockingbird* was originally called only *Atticus*. F. Scott Fitzgerald's *The Great Gatsby* was titled *Trimalchio in West Egg* and *Portnoy's Complaint* allegedly was *The Jewboy, Wacking Off*.

6. **Map Out the Main Players:** Since drama/conflict/tension fuels most fiction, it often helps to delineate who your major dramatic conflict is between. My novels were centered around a romantic relationship gone horribly wrong, the clashes between two women who switched lives, and the frustration of a woman simultaneously feeling abandoned by her husband, therapist and best friend. Some authors first pick their players and do a short character sketch, and only then imagine what struggles they might live through. "What helps me is to start by inventing the characters I really want to spend time with," said my former student David Goodwillie, author of *American Subversive* (2010) and *King's County* (2020). "I enjoy not quite knowing where a novel is going plot-wise, trusting that it'll be somewhere interesting because I've created complex people. I put them in intriguing situations, where the stakes are high and choices need to be made. Often I find my characters make the choices for me. I don't think of the big picture—the years it will take to write, edit or sell. I just think each day of furthering the story of my characters, an intriguing challenge to look forward to."

7. **What Story Are You Telling?** You want to share the saga that only you can tell. If you are having trouble conjuring up a plot, consider mining your own life for anything funny, painful or dramatic you can make into art. In my case, I have no imagination, so reality was my inspiration. After my New York girlfriend married my brother, moved to Michigan, had four kids like my mom and became the daughter my mother always wanted, I complained to my shrink. Then I thought: *Hey, this would make a good novel.* It became *Overexposed.* Another time when I bumped into an old professor I'd briefly dated who didn't remember me, I ran to my shrink freaking out. (Yes I'm aware of the pattern.) I was fascinated to consider

that my ex might still be angry thirty years later. This inspired my indie novel *What's Never Said*. When my shrink relocated, I needed his replacement. He charged $200 a session while the therapists on my new insurance cost only $25 co-pay. So I decided to see eight shrinks in eight days. Instead of Speed Dating, I was *Speed Shrinking*, a concept I turned into a comic novel.

Many modern hits—like Nora Ephron's 1983 *Heart Burn* and Justin Torres's *We the Animals* (2011)—mirror actual events. When another one-time student Daniela Petrova—who'd struggled with infertility for years—tried a donor-egg cycle, she imagined it as the premise for her fascinating 2019 novel *Her Daughter's Mother*. What if a woman who gets pregnant with an egg donor wants to meet the younger girl and stalks her to find out more about the genes her baby would inherit? If the biological donor vanishes, could the pregnant woman be a suspect? Something that really happened can inspire great fiction.

8. **Decide Who Gets to Tell It:** There are many ways to relate the drama you've chosen to your reader. You could employ first-person, using a voice that's inside the head of one protagonist/hero/main character like the aforementioned *Catcher in the Rye* ("If you really want to hear about it, the first thing you'll probably want to know is where I was born, and what my lousy childhood was like . . ."). Another choice is an omnipotent narrator that George Orwell used in his 1945 allegorical novel *Animal Farm* ("Mr. Jones, of the Manor Farm, had locked the hen-houses for the night, but was too drunk to remember to shut the pop-holes. With the ring of light from his lantern dancing from side to side, he lurched across the yard . . .").

A third-person narrator could be in the head of one character at a time, as in *The Game of Thrones*. George R.R. Martin starts each section of each of his most famous fictional series with the name of the persona telling their point of view—alternating between Bran Stark, Eddard Stark, Catelyn Stark, Jon Snow, Daenerys Targaryen,

Tyrion Lannister, Arya Stark, Sansa Stark and more—a great, easy way to indicate who is speaking when.

Petrova's *Her Daughter's Mother* did this while switching off sections between her three main characters: the thirty-eight-year-old infertile heroine Lana, Tyler—her off-and-on boyfriend who fathered the child, and their twenty-one-year-old egg donor Katya. Learning new facts and secrets from three sides worked especially well in this slowly unraveling mystery.

9. **Don't Begin at the Beginning:** "A big mistake I see is authors starting way too soon. We don't need to know someone's childhood up until the point they became a master jewel thief," Leavitt said. "Begin with the conflict, show that jewel thief creeping on a rooftop to steal a diamond, and then, maybe when she goes into the room, there's a rocking chair that triggers a memory of her parents tying her to a rocking chair because she was bad." Launch your novel dramatically by showing action, with your character about to fall off a cliff (literally or metaphorically). Once you grab us, we'll care more about their childhood.

Students often cite great books that defy this suggestion. Yes, *The Life and Opinions of Tristram Shandy, Gentleman* by Laurence Sterne (1759) begins before his hero was born and Daniel Defoe's 1719 *Robinson Crusoe* and Dickens's *David Copperfield* (1850) also commence with the protagonist's first breath. Yet since birth is taken, I wouldn't try to replicate it as a lead without great reason, as in Salman Rushdie's *Midnight's Children* (1981), where the hero is born at the inception of India, or Jeffrey Eugenides's 2002 *Middlesex,* which has a trans narrator ("I was born twice: first, as a baby girl, on a remarkably smog-less Detroit day in January of 1960; and then again, as a teenager boy, in an emergency room near Petoskey, Michigan, in August of 1974."). Louise Erdrich's 2017 Dystopian thriller *Future Home of the Living God* twists the conceit with the adopted pregnant heroine going to meet her biological family.

10. **Study Your Favorite Novels, Underline and Take Notes:** If you're confused about structure, reread books you admired to see how the authors did it. Petrova took a bestseller in her genre that she loved—*Girl on the Train*—and dissected it into pieces. "When does the inciting incident occur? What happens at the midpoint? When are there moments of reflection?" she asked. "This approach was helpful to me when trying to figure out how to pace a suspense novel . . . In different colors I highlighted description paragraphs, sections devoted to characters' introspection, action and dialogue segments to get a sense of the ratio between these elements. Then I highlighted my manuscript and looked at each chapter to make sure I had a good balance between description, action and dialogue. It helped me identify scenes where I'd failed to explain important feelings or motivations." By combining a successful structure with her own idiosyncratic story, Petrova came up with a winner.

    But be careful not to lose your voice in someone else's. Leavitt once spent months reading D.H. Lawrence and when she began her next novel, guess who she sounded like? "The biggest mistake aspiring novelists make is: trying to be like someone else. Be unique," Leavitt said. "Ask yourself: What was haunting me that I had to write this particular story? What's the question I want to find an answer to as I'm writing this novel?"

11. **Commit to a Writing Schedule:** Will this be a full-time undertaking or something you do part time in between other employment? Because I taught at night, I was able to make writing my book a full-time day job where I usually commit to waking up and writing at least 300 words daily. You need to find a time and space where you won't be interrupted or distracted. For those who don't have an office or room with a door you can shut, consider renting a writer's space like Paragraph in New York, L.A.'s Unique Space or Soho House (which has many locations from London to Miami). If you're broke, try a coffee shop, park or local library.

12. **Find Ways to Get Smart Criticism:** After finishing chapter one (mine average 10 pages), don't send it to an agent or book editor. Instead, beg someone you trust to read it—especially a teacher, mentor or published author—and ask what they think. This is not a small request. They are doing you a big favor. So if they say yes, give them time to do it. If they offer feedback, don't argue or speak, just listen and take notes. Don't wait to complete a whole book before getting feedback from experts. You don't want to find out you're not on a good track after you wasted a year or two going in the wrong direction for 375 pages. If you can't take a class, consider hiring a ghost editor, ideally a former editor or an agent who will tell you what's working best and least. While an editor will charge you (prices vary), a reputable literary agent will only take a percentage of work they sell. (If they ask for money up front, try a different agent).

If you can't afford a class or a ghost editor, start a free writing workshop with colleagues (in person or online) to give you dead-lines to hand in pages. While members or students' feedback won't be as precise as the criticism of established professionals, if a dozen people in your group find your second paragraph better than the first, I'd try it their way.

"But do not ask for a critique from people who love you," warns Leavitt. "They won't be critical enough. Even more, they won't know how to fix what is wrong. Maybe find a writing partner where you can share pages, because being able to critique someone else's novel will help you figure out your own work." Leavitt, who also does freelance editing on the side (using the term "develop-mental editor" over "ghost editor" or "book doctor"), says most of the books she edits don't work at first because they don't have the right skeleton and structure—which you might need an expert to help you figure out.

"Your work doesn't haven't to be perfect—or even close to perfect—in the first, second or third drafts," adds Goodwillie. "Real writing is rewriting, part of the process successful writers look forward to with delight. The music of the language always comes late in the process. Give the orchestra plenty of time to warm up."

AN ARGUMENT FOR FIRST-PERSON PAST TENSE

Who will tell your story? The point of view you'll be using is essential to figure out on page 1, as well as which tense you'll employ. Students who have yet to publish their work have shown me pages from their novels-in-progress where they've experimented with forms, viewpoints, time and narration. One tried second-person present: "When you walk into the room, you know this sucks."

Someone ambitiously attempted second-person future: "You will be reading this on the train tomorrow, not knowing it will be your last day on earth."

Another used third-person present: "David does not understand why Lisa is gone."

One attempted a present-tense epistolary novel told completely through texts, filled with emojis and initialisms: "OMG get your hot ass over here, baby needs a byc now LOL . . . " ("byc" was slang for Booty Call apparently.)

They were all interesting and I'm all for creativity and originality. Yet the farther from the norm you travel, the higher the bar will be for excellence, and the harder it will be to get paid and published. In my case, I wanted to simplify the process.

When I went back to reread the favorite novels on my shelves, I realized that almost all the fiction I loved was in first-person past tense. This was true for international literary gems, modern triumphs and commercial fun. When it came to publishing novels myself, I found first-person past tense to be the easiest and most common way to tell a story. It felt like the most honest and understandable too, since I was indeed the one recounting the story to the reader.

Here are the beginnings of twelve first-person past-tense novels that inspired me (though a few employ other tenses too). I'm sharing them to suggest why—if you aren't sure or are debating—you might begin your book emulating this clean and classy narration choice.

"You will rejoice to hear that no disaster has accompanied the commencement of an enterprise which you have regarded with such evil forebodings. I arrived here yesterday; and my first task is to assure my dear sister of my welfare, and increasing confidence in the success of my undertaking." *Frankenstein* by Mary Shelley (1818)

"In my younger and more vulnerable years my father gave me some advice that I've been turning over in my mind ever since. 'Whenever you feel like criticizing anyone,' he told me, 'just remember that all the people in this world haven't had the advantages that you've had.'" *The Great Gatsby* by F. Scott Fitzgerald (1925)

"In the last summer of that year we lived in a house in a village that looked across the river and the plain to the mountains. In the bed of the river there were pebbles and boulders, dry and white in the sun, and the water was clear and swiftly moving and blue in the channels. Troops went by the house and down the road and the dust they raised powdered the leaves of the trees." *A Farewell to Arms* by Ernest Hemingway (1929)

"Mother died today. Or, maybe, yesterday; I can't be sure. The telegram from Home says: YOUR MOTHER PASSED AWAY. FUNERAL TOMORROW. DEEP SYMPATHY. Which leaves the matter doubtful; it could have been yesterday." *The Stranger* by Albert Camus (1942)

"She was so deeply imbedded in my consciousness that for the first year of school I seem to have believed that each of my teachers was my mother in disguise. As soon as the last bell had sounded, I would rush off for home, wondering as I ran if I could possibly make it to our apartment before she had succeeded in transforming herself." *Portnoy's Complaint* by Philip Roth (1969)

"There were 117 psychoanalysts on the Pan Am flight to Vienna and I'd been treated by at least six of them. And married a seventh." *Fear of Flying* by Erica Jong (1973)

"I was born in the city of Bombay…once upon a time. No, that won't do, there's no getting away from the date: I was born in Doctor Narlikar's Nursing Home on August 15, 1947. And the time? The time matters, too. Well then: at night. No, it's important to be more…On the stroke of midnight, as a matter of fact. Clock-hands joined palms in respectful greeting as I came. Oh spell it out, spell it out: at the precise instance of India's arrival at independence, I tumbled forth into the world." *Midnight's Children* by Salman Rushdie (1980)

"We didn't always live on Mango Street. Before that we lived on Looms on the third floor, and before that we lived on Keeler. Before Keeler it was Paulina, and before that I can't remember. But what I remember most is moving a lot. Each time it seemed there'd be one more of us. By the time we got to Mango Street there were six—Mama, Papa, Carlos, Kiki, my sister Nenny and me." *The House on Mango Street* by Sandra Cisneros (1983)

"My mother started the San Francisco version of the Joy Luck Club in 1949, two years before I was born. This was the year my mother and father left China with one stiff leather trunk filled only with fancy silk dresses. There was no time to pack anything else, my mother had explained to my father after they boarded the boat…" *The Joy Luck Club* by Amy Tan (1989)

"I was surprised to see a white man walk into Joppy's bar. It's not just that he wore white but he wore an off-white linen suit and shirt with a Panama straw hat and bone shoes over flashing white silk socks." *Devil in a Blue Dress* by Walter Mosley (1990)

"Lifetimes ago, under a banyan tree in the village of Hasnapur, an astrologer cupped his ears—his satellite dish to the stars—and foretold my widowhood and exile. I was only seven then, fast and venturesome, scabrous-armed from leaves and thorns." *Jasmine* by Bharati Mukherjee (1990)

"Once upon a time, in a far-off land, I was kidnapped by a gang of fearless yet terrified young men with so much impossible hope beating inside their bodies it burned their very skin and strengthened their will right through the bones. They held me captive for thirteen days. They wanted to break me. It was not personal. I was not broken." *An Untamed State* by Roxane Gay (2014)

THIRD-PERSON PAST TENSE

"It was love at first sight. The first time Yossarian saw the chaplain he fell madly in love with him. Yossarian was in the hospital with a pain in his liver that fell just short of being jaundice. The doctors were puzzled by the fact that it wasn't quite jaundice." *Catch 22* by Joseph Heller (1955)

"Sometimes Sonny felt like he was the only human creature in the town. It was a bad feeling, and it usually came on him in the mornings early, when the streets were completely empty, the way they were one Saturday morning in late November." *The Last Picture Show* by Larry McMurtry (1966)

"The book was thick and black and covered with dust. Its boards were bowed and creaking; it had been maltreated in its own time. Its spine was missing, or, rather, protruded from amongst the leaves like a bulky marker. It was bandaged about and about with dirty white tape, tied in a neat bow. The librarian handed it to Roland Mitchell, who was sitting waiting for it in the Reading Room of the London Library." *Possession* by A.S. Byatt (1990)

SECOND-PERSON PRESENT TENSE

"You are not the kind of guy who would be at a place like this at this time of the morning. But here you are, and you cannot say the terrain is entirely unfamiliar, although the details are fuzzy. You are at a nightclub taking to a girl with a shaved head." *Bright Lights, Big City* by Jay McInerney (1984)

FIRST-PERSON PRESENT TENSE

"I stand at the window of this great house in the south of France as night falls, the night which is leading me to the most terrible morning of my life. I have a drink in my hand, there is a bottle at my elbow. I watch my reflection in the darkening gleam of the window pane. My reflection is tall, perhaps rather like an arrow, my blond hair glows. My face is like a face you have seen many times." *Giovanni's Room* by James Baldin (1956)

"Here is Sofka, in a wedding photograph; at least, I assume it is a wedding, although the bride and groom are absent. Sofka stands straight and stern, her shoulders braced, her head erect in the manner of two generations earlier." *Family and Friends* by Anita Brookner (1998)

EXPERT ADVICE: A NOVELIST WHO EDITS NOVELS

Whenever I need a fun panelist or speaker, I ask Rakesh Satyal, a gregarious book editor who has edited fiction and nonfiction at Random House, HarperCollins and Simon and Schuster. He's also been an NYU teacher, a cabaret singer and an acclaimed novelist himself. His debut *Blue Boy* (2010) won awards from the Association of Asian American Studies, the Publishing Triangle and Lambda Literary where, in lieu of a traditional acceptance speech, he sang his thanks to the music of Lady Gaga's "Bad Romance." For his second novel *No One Can Pronounce My Name* (2017), he took to YouTube in a red velvet cape to sing "Buy My Book" to the tune of King George's "You'll Be Back" from Hamilton, and wound up on Seth Meyers. Yet he's more apt to show off about the authors he edits, including such talented queer voices as Janet Mock, Armistead Maupin, Paul Rudnick, Terry Castle and Vestal McIntyre. He's proud of the recent novels Bisi Adjapon's *Of Women and Frogs* (2019), Evan James's *Cheer Up, Mr. Widdicome* (2019) and Tiffanie Tsao's *The Majesties* (2020). Since he's been on dual sides of fiction deals, I asked Satyal to share some inside routes to being a successful novelist.

1. **Look for Full-Time Publishing Jobs:** Rakesh's college professor Joyce Carol Oates noticed he was a good critic and suggested he try book publishing—the way Toni Morrison, E.L. Doctorow

and Edmund White began their careers. Many people start with low-paying assistant jobs (if not in editorial, then in publicity) and work their way up. Being an insider at a literary agency or book publisher demystifies the biz since you get to see every stage of how the sausages are made. You get a steady paycheck, health insurance, a safety net and lots of free books. Yet you have to give your day job the respect it deserves, Satyal said, and not just treat it as a short-term stepping stone.

2. **Separate Church and State:** To compartmentalize his double careers as writer and editor, Satyal sold his novels to different publishers. During his 9 to 5 job, now as an executive editor at Atria, he makes a point to focus only on the work of his authors. While seeing both sides helps him be more empathetic with writers, he does not bring up his life as an author when he has his editor hat on.

3. **Learn the Business Side:** If you don't want to be an editor or agent, at least go to panels and conferences and ask a lot of questions about how advances and royalties work. In medicine, law or business, students are taught to be well-versed in their industries. Although writing can be an art, understanding the finances of the field will better prime you for the often turbulent life of an author.

4. **Don't Be an Island:** Satyal's husband is a literary agent who reads early drafts of his work, his brother is a stand-up comic and many of his friends and colleagues are in publishing and entertainment. Though some people don't want their world to be as insular, it's hard to write, edit and publish on your own. Enroll in an MFA program, take classes or join organizations like the Authors Guild, NBCC or ASJA. Satyal has served on the advisory committee for PEN American Center's annual World Voices Festival and he's been a vice president of Lambda Literary, which champions LGBTQ voices. Having a shared community makes a literary life much more attainable—and sustainable.

5. **Carve Out Time and Space:** Finishing a novel can take years. Working full time, Satyal focuses on his own books on weekends,

nights and on his lunch hour. He's been willing to give up social life, vacations and leisure activities to pursue his vision. It can be tiring and draining. Remember: successful people do what others won't do to get ahead.

6. **Be Careful with Other Races and Cultures:** While Satyal agrees with the principle, crafting multicultural characters who don't look or sound like you is hard to pull off. These days you can't do it flippantly, or for superficial or commercial reasons. Instead of throwing in different-colored characters in the mix for the sake of diversity, do the hard work of reading many books by authors of the group you're trying to depict. Take classes and study with professors from varied backgrounds. Hire sensitivity readers and listen to their advice. Be respectful of other worldviews.

7. **Don't Be a Ventriloquist:** It's smart to read the most award-winning bestselling novels in your category. Yet be careful you don't copy someone else's voice, style or subject matter. Don't jump on a trend or try to emulate what's popular now. From the time it's sold until it comes out, a novel can take eighteen months or two years and by that time something else will be trending. You're better off writing something that only you can write, that's genuine, from your heart.

EXPERT ADVICE ON THE STORY BEHIND SHORT STORIES

Moderating a publishing panel at New York University not long ago, I told the audience, "Novels are much easier to sell than short story collections and get much bigger advances from better houses." I was repeating advice I'd heard from book editors over the years—so common it was cliché. "Not so," countered my colleague, agent Renée Zuckerbrot. "I love books of short stories and just sold one at auction to a major publisher for six figures." It turned out the former book editor turned literary agent is a short story aficionado, with tastes that run from the older masters John Cheever, Alice Monroe and Debra Eisenberg to ZZ Packer, Bryan Washington and Carmen

Maria Machado. Zuckerbrot has single-handedly sold a dozen great collections for her clients to a range of publishers from Milkweed and Tin House to HarperCollins and Random House, for advances between $7,500 and well into the six figures. These include Shawn Vestal's *Godforsaken Idaho* (2013), Kelly Link's *Get In Trouble* (2015) and Polly Rosenwaike's *Look How Happy I'm Making You* (2019). Here's her inside scoop on how sell a book of short stories.

1. **Fund the Field:** If you want literary journals and book houses to keep publishing short stories, support them by purchasing the journals and book collections. If you can't afford a hardcover, buy a paperback or e-book. If you're broke, use the library. If you love it, post rave reviews on Amazon, Goodreads and BarnesandNoble. com and repost the good press on Twitter, Facebook and Instagram, recommending the book to others to be generous.

2. **Get In Print:** It's rare that someone who has never been published before will land a book deal for short stories—unless you're famous like actors Tom Hanks, B.J. Novak, Jesse Eisenberg or filmmaker Miranda July. For mere mortals, it's best to have three to five short stories published if you want an editor to pay you an advance for short stories.

3. **To Land an Agent, Finish Something:** It could be a completed collection, which is usually nine to twelve stories. Or you could submit a few finished stories along with an entire novel, which might lead you to a two-book deal.

4. **Your Stories Have Two Jobs:** Each one should stand alone so it can be published in its entirety in a magazine or journal. Plus, in a collection, the stories should also be in conversation with each other. Short fiction in *The New Yorker* averages between 5,000 and 10,000 words, though flash fiction can be 500 words or fewer. The mind-blowing Lydia Davis has stories from one sentence long to 40 pages, while Israeli author Etgar Keret has published dazzling surrealistic stories as short as 1 page. (To improve your work and

chances, consider taking a class or joining a free writing workshop for feedback or hire a ghost editor who specializes in this kind of abbreviated fiction.)

5. **Collections Need Connections:** David Schickler's *Kissing in Manhattan* (2001) links stories about three love-hungry urbanites who live in the same Manhattan apartment building. Elizabeth Strout's *Olive Kitteridge* (made into an HBO series) offers thirteen stories about the difficult title character in the coastal town of Crosby, Maine. Aesthetics and tone can link a collection, like Kelly Link's nine stories in *Get In Trouble* (2015), a finalist for the Pulitzer Prize for fiction, which mix fantasy, magical realism and horror. Also brilliant and genre-bending is Carmen Maria Machado's award-winning caustic, queer and sexy collection *Her Body and Other Parties* (2017). Bryan Washington's *Lot* follows, among many characters, a gay biracial working class young man in Houston searching for community.

6. **Try the Big Guns:** Selling a story to *The New Yorker, Harper's Magazine, The Atlantic, Paris Review* or *Granta* can greatly enhance your odds of selling a whole collection, especially if your work goes viral. After "Cat Person," about a creepy sexual encounter, ran in *The New Yorker* in 2017—the height of the #MeToo movement— and caused a huge stir, the thirty-six-year-old Kristen Roupenian received a seven-figure book deal for her debut *You Know You Want This* (2019) and an unwritten novel.

7. **Literary Journals Count Too:** There are many prestigious magazines and journals that agents and book editors peruse, including *A Public Space, Zoetrope, One Story, N+1, The Sun, Slice, American Short Fiction, Bomb* and *Zyzzyva*. And don't forget the quarterlies: *Michigan Quarterly, Iowa, Missouri, Sewanee, Kenyan, Virginia, New England, Southern* or *Three Penny Review.* You can find an extensive database of literary journals and quarterlies in the back of *Poets and Writers.* "Each one has its own aesthetic and focus," Zuckerbrot advised. "So read them carefully before submitting."

CHAPTER 9

Genre Fiction

FIGURING OUT FICTIONAL SUBGROUPS

Once referred to as "dime novels" or "pulp fiction," genre fiction is an umbrella term that describes popular entertaining commercial works of imagination under headings like crime, suspense or horror. For decades they were published as mass market paperbacks, produced cheaply for wide audiences. Today they can also be found in hardcover, trade, and e-books. They appeal largely to a niche audience who are already fans of the category. Emphasizing plot over literary prowess, they've been known to spawn many sequels featuring the same predicable structure and protagonist, like a weekly TV show, which explains why so many book series wind up filmed on both the big and small screens. Many bestselling authors in all categories began careers in genre fiction.

Famous series include Walter Mosley's five Easy Rawlins mysteries about a Black detective facing racism in L.A., Jeannie Lin's Harlequin romantic histories set in Tang Dynasty China, George R.R. Martin's *Game of Thrones* fantasy sci-fi saga, Daniel Silva's twenty spy thrillers about a former Israel intelligence operative and the *Twilight* vampire romance books by Stephanie Meyers that sold 100 million copies.

In some circles, genre fiction is considered artistically inferior to literary fiction, more colloquial, literal and breezy. It's easier to read, with less complex symbolism, allusions and experimentation, which is perhaps why it's more popular with masses of readers. University curricula are more apt to study literary books while Netflix will buy more genre fiction. A *Writer's Digest* article suggested you ask yourself, "Is my book more likely to be read in college English classes or in a grocery checkout line?"

Keep in mind that boundaries are bendable and the "literary" label can cross over. A professor colleague I admire teaches an entire class on Don DeLillo, whose bestsellers incorporate elements of mystery, crime and espionage. Michael Chabon's Pulitzer Prize–winning *The Amazing Adventures of Kavalier and Clay* (2000) mixes history, Jewish mysticism and comics, while his *The Yiddish Policeman's Union* (2007) is a detective story set in an alternative universe that won the science fiction awards the Nebula, the Hugo and the Locus, and was shortlisted for the Edgar Allen Poe best mystery prize. British author Sophie Hannah published acclaimed poetry books, self-help, bestselling crime, mysteries and domestic thrillers and helped launched a Master's Degree in Crime and Thriller Writing at the University of Cambridge.

Whether your book is literary, mainstream or belongs in a genre subgroup depends on your audience, readers' expectations and external frames that help publishers sell more copies. If an agent wants literary and commercial fiction but not genre fiction, that usually means they want books with broader appeal. While any novel could have elements of romance or mystery, picture which bookstore shelf your title will inhabit. Would it be general fiction or in the mystery, sci-fi, horror or romance sections? While it's still competitive to break into, it's often easier to sell multiple books of genre fiction than commercial or literary novels, since they tend to follow a simple formula, pay less and publish much faster. Many bestselling prolific authors have been known to crank out several books a year, using pseudonyms for different series so as not to flood the market, like Nora Roberts/J.D. Robb.

The biggest challenge for aspiring authors may be deciding which category your project will fall under. "That's because the labels are constantly changing and many are overlapping," said Shannon Jamieson

Vazquez, who has been an acclaimed book editor at such publishers as Bantam Dell, Berkley NAL, Crooked Lane and Little Brown. Diana Gabaldon's *Outlander* series (a sweeping time-travel saga and now a TV show I've binge-watched), might be considered romance, fantasy, speculative, magical realism and/or historical fiction, she pointed out. Stephen King is filed under mystery, crime, thriller, police procedural, horror, science-fiction, paranormal or fantasy, depending on which book, year and who you ask. Romance is a huge division within itself with layers of specializations that incorporate other genres, such as paranormal, suspense, sci-fi or historical.

The first step to success in this crowded field is getting yourself up-to-date on what's out there. There's a good chance the idea you think is so original has been done before. For example, if an author coming up with a story involving a woman werewolf Googled "female werewolf books," they would instantly find dozens, including Kelly Armstrong's *Bitten* (2001), the first book in her Women of the Otherworld series, which led to thirty-one bestsellers over the last twenty years.

The most common rookie mistake aspiring writers make, warned Vazquez, is not reading enough and assuming they know what's going on in their field. "That sets you up to not be taken seriously because you haven't paid enough attention to what's out there now," Vazquez said. "If an author claims to be breaking new territory with an Urban Fantasy novel and never mentions how it's different from #1 *New York Times* bestselling authors in that category Ilona Andrews, Kim Harrison or Laurell K. Hamilton, it tells me they don't know the market."

To get a quick education, read many recent novels like yours. An agent, book editor or publishing marketer might later weigh in on how your book will ultimately be labelled. Yet it's smarter for you to get a strong sense of where your project belongs, if for no other reason than you won't be able to approach the right agent and editors if you don't know who to approach and how they are differentiated. (If you're up a tree, take a fiction class or seminar, ask a writing teacher, a novelist who has published in your subcategory, fellow student or colleague for their opinion. For more direction, you can a hire a ghost editor who specializes in genre fiction, as Vazquez used to do.)

Here are the top nine categories bought by the mainstream publishers I spoke with. Yes, I mention some very old, classic, famous and/or noteworthy books from each niche (versus what's out next season) and I shamelessly plug the books of former students and personal favorites. Though many subgenres overlap, I (subjectively) chose only one category for each book based on descriptions in reviews and publishing catalogues. I focused mainly on adult books, since middle-grade and young adult often need a specific agent, editor and division that may not sell books for adult readers. And I reductively include TV and movie adaptations for their name recognition to help writers immediately get the picture (as in "Oh *Psych* and *Monk*, yeah those are goofy detectives"). Most of the screen adaptations started as book series, like Lee Goldberg's sixteen *Monk* novels about a detective with OCD beginning with *Mr. Monk Goes to the Firehouse* (2006). A few became books *after* their TV/film popularity, like William Rabkin's series on the police consultant who pretends to be psychic: *Psych: A Mind Is a Terrible Thing to Read* (2009).

1. **Mystery:** These "Whodunits" usually present a puzzle that revolves around solving a crime that happens at the start. Potential suspects are revealed early on and there's little on-stage violence. They are subdivided by publishers under: cozy, amateur sleuth, procedural and crime and average between 60,000 and 80,000 words.

    A. Cozy means the characters are more important than the crime. Sex, violence and gore are off stage. It's all wrapped up at the end and can be humorous. Because of this lighter touch, the are many more female authors and readers.

    International Classics: Agatha Christie's first *The Mysterious Affair at Styles* (1920) and Welsh author Edward Marston's Elizabethan Theatre series started with *The Queen's Head* (1988)

Comic: Michael Bond's *Monsieur Pamplemousse* (1986) series involves a dog named Pomme Frites and Rita Mae Brown's *Wish You Were Here* (1990), the first of thirty Sneaky Pie Brown mysteries solved with a pet cat named Sneaky Pie

B. Amateur Sleuth is where the character—or someone other than the police—tries to solve the crime. They are similar to cozies but can be racier.

Old Screen Classic: Raymond Chandler's *Farewell My Lovely* (1940)

More Contemporary Hit: Laura Lippman's *Charm City* (1997), the first of twelve about reporter Tess Monaghan, and *Assault with a Deadly Lie* (2014) by Lev Raphael, one in a series of eight books about Nick Hoffman, a Midwest gay Jewish professor, like its author

International Hit: Naomi Hirahara's *Summer of the Big Bachi* (2004) about a Japanese-American gardener in L.A.

C. Procedurals: This subgenre emphasizes the investigative protocols of a police officer, FBI, CIA or other official department rather than a private detective or amateur sleuth.

Early Classic: Ed McBaine's *87th Precinct* series (1956)

Screen Hit: *The Black Echo* by Michael Connelly (1992), which became the *Bosch* TV show

International Hits: Chinese poet-author Qiu Xiaolong's *Death of a Red Heroine* (2001), *Still Life* by Canadian writer Louise Penny (2005) and Irish author Tara French's *In the Woods* (2007)

Personal Favorite: *Devil in a Blue Dress* by Walter Mosley (1990)

D. Crime: These are grittier and focus on criminals and victims more than law enforcement.

Recent Hit: Steph Cha's *Your House Will Pay* (2019)

International Hit: Japanese author Natsuo Kirino's *Out* (1997).

Personal Favorite: Elmore Leonard's *City Primeval*, later called *High Noon in Detroit* (1980), and *Out of Sight* (1996), made into the best Jennifer Lopez movie

2. **Suspense:** In this arena, the worry and anticipation about impending danger is high because the reader is usually aware of things that the hero is not.

Most Famous (mostly male) Bestsellers: Robert Ludlum, Ken Follett, Harlan Coben, Lee Child, John Grisham, James Patterson, Dan Brown, Dean Koontz, Tom Clancy and Scott Turow

Recent Screen Hits: Liane Moriarty's *Big Little Lies* (2014), Paula Hawkin's *Girl on the Train* (2015), Gillian Flynn's *Sharp Objects* (2006) and *Gone Girl* (2012), and Celeste Ng's *Little Fires Everywhere* (2017)

Marketing Ploy: More suspenseful books with *Girl* in the title: Erik Axl Sund's *The Crow Girl* (2010), *Shining Girls* by Lauren Beukes (2013), Mary Kubica's *The Good Girl* (2014), Sandra Block's *The Girl Without a Name* (2015), *Boring Girls* by Sara Taylor (2015), Karen Slaughter's *Pretty Girls* (2015), Marion Pauw's *Girl in the Dark* (2016) and Nina Laurin's *Girl Last Seen* (2017)

International Hit Trilogy that launched the *Girl* Craze: Swede Stieg Larsson's *The Girl with the Dragon Tattoo* (2005), *The Girl Who Played with Fire* (2006,) and *The Girl Who Kicked the Hornet's Nest* (2007), all published after Larsson died.

Variation: A.J. Finn, a.k.a. Daniel Mallory with *Woman in the Window* (2018)

3. **Thrillers:** Dark and scary, these books are characterized by heightened fear, surprise and anxiety, the way you feel at a Hitchcock movie. The main dramatic event occurs in the middle, at the end, or keeps happening. There are spy, action, crime, legal, medical, political, eco, psychological and military thrillers. They usually center on a hero haunted by a villain who is committing multiple crimes with more than one victim, which is why serial killers are a popular theme.

Classics: Patricia Highsmith's *Strangers on a Train* (1950) and *The Spy Who Came in from the Cold* by John le Carré (1963)

International Hit Series: Norwegian author Jo Nesbo's *The Leopard* (1960) followed by *The Bat,* which became thirteen Harry

Hole books, and the Scottish Val McDermid's *Report for Murder* (1987), the first of five books in a series about Lindsay Gordon, a self-proclaimed "cynical social lesbian feminist journalist"

American Screen Hit: *Silence of the Lambs* by Thomas Harris (1988)

More Recent Screen Hit: *The Gray Man* by Mark Greaney (2009), the first of ten books about a former CIA operative now a killer for hire, a Netflix movie and, they hope, a blockbuster franchise.

Note: Mystery, crime and thrillers often have their own publishers and imprints, so check out Mulholland Books, Crooked Lane, Jove, Endeavor Press, Felony and Mayhem, Hard Case Crime, Brash Books, Alibi, Henery Press, Joffe Books, Lyrical Press, Level Best, Minotaur, Alibi and Seventh Street.

4. **Science Fiction:** Imaginative, scientific and futuristic concepts can focus on space exploration, parallel universes, extraterrestrial life or utopian or dystopian worlds. Publishers break it down into speculative, hard sci-fi and space opera, along with such recent subgenres as post-apoc, solarpunk and afrofuturism (which often cross over into fantastic literature). Sci-fi and fantasy books tend to be longer lately, between 90,000 and 150,000 words. Big fantasy and sci-fi publishers are Hydra, Del Rey, Ace, Tor, Roc, Orbit, Falstaff Books, Luna Press and Apex.

A. Classic Speculative Sci-Fi: This involves imagined technologies that don't exist in the actual world, like *Starship Troopers* by Robert A. Heinlein (1959), who defined the term in 1947 and said most stories fit into: The Gadget Story, The Human Interest Story, Boy Meets Girl, The Little Tailor, or The Main Who Learned Better. Interestingly, his first Utopian novel *For Us, the Living* did not see print in his lifetime.

Most Prolific: Isaac Asimov published more than one hundred books, starting with *Pebble in the Sky* (1950). Philip K. Dick had 121 short stories and forty-four novels out, including *The Man in the*

High Castle (1962) and *Do Androids Dream of Electric Sheep?* (1968) (which became the film *Blade Runner* and the story *We Can Remember It for Your Wholesale*, which inspired the movie *Total Recall*).

B. Hard SF exists within the realm of scientific possibility and is not outside the known physical laws of the universe. There is often an emphasis on accuracy—think Arthur C. Clarke's *The Fountains of Paradise* (1979) about the construction of a space elevator linking with a satellite. *Jurassic Park* by Michael Crichton (1990), which inspired the movie, is about an amusement park/zoo with genetically recreated dinosaurs that accidentally come to life, said to be a cautionary tale about genetic engineering.

C. Epic Space Opera: This subgenre revolves around space warfare, melodramatic adventure and interplanetary battles. Consider *Star Wars* (1976), which was ghost written by Alan Dean Foster but credited to George Lucas and came out months before the film that led to sixteen books by different authors.

Feminist breakthroughs: *The Left Hand of Darkness* by Ursula K. Le Guin (1969) and *Kindred* by Octavia Butler (1979)

More Contemporary Hit: *Empire of Light* (2019) by Alex Harrow, the first very queer futurist sci-fi fantasy series characters by a queer and nonbinary author whose pronouns are they/them

5. **Horror/Paranormal:** The raison d'être for this subgenre is to scare, frighten, disgust or startle readers with terror, often from supernatural element like zombies, ghosts, vampires, werewolves, aliens, haunted houses or family curses. Publishers with apt names include Severed Press, Night Shade and Dark Moon Books.

Literary Classic: Mary Shelley's *Frankenstein* (1818)

Screen Hits: Stephen King's *The Shining* (1977) and *Silence of the Lambs* by Thomas Harris (1988)

Huge Hits by Women Authors: Anne Rice's gothic horror *Interview with a Vampire* (1976) led to ten novels in the Vampire Chronicles, and Karen Slaughter's *Blindsighted* (2001) has sold 35 million copies in thirty-seven different languages. Carmen Maria

Machado's *Her Body and Other Parties* (2017) and *My Body, Herself* (2019) are a mix of LGBT, horror and sci-fiction. Her *The Low, Low Woods* (2020) is an experimental scary mystery graphic comic novel.

6. **Fantasy/Speculative:** In these imaginary, sometimes dystopian universes, supernatural and magical creatures mingle with realistic people. These plots could not occur in real life.

   High Fantasy Classics: *Lord of the Rings* by J.R.R. Tolkien (1954) and *A Song of Ice and Fire* series by George R.R. Martin (1996), which became HBO's *Game of Thrones*

   Contemporary Fantasy: Connie Willis's *Blackout* (2010)

   Urban Fantasy: Kelley Armstrong's *Bitten* (2001) and Charlaine Harris's *Dead Until Dark* (2001), a Sookie Stackhouse book that led to HBO's *True Blood*

7. **Romance:** The primary focus here is a love relationship and it usually has a happy ending. There are many mainstream and literary romantic novels, from Jane Austen's *Pride and Prejudice* (1813) to Nicholas Sparks's *The Notebook* (1996). Yet in genre fiction this refers to formulaic plots, mostly by female authors, from such niche publishers and imprints as Harlequin, Avon, Entangled, Lyrical Press, Loveswept, Flirt, Forever Yours, Swerve, Bookouture and Limitless.

   A. Erotica: E. L. James's *Fifty Shades of Grey* (2011) that led to a series and movies and *Reverb* (2019), one in a series of romance books "for all colors of the rainbow" by Anna Zabo, who uses they/them pronouns. It's out from Carina Press, Harlequin's digital-first adult fiction imprint.

   B. Historical Romance: Regency is the largest subgenre. *Potent Pleasures* (1999), which became a trilogy, led to thirty more best-selling books by Eloise James, the pen name of Fordham University Shakespeare professor Mary Bly.

   C. Contemporary Romance: *Angel's Fall (2006)* by Nora Roberts, author of two hundred novels

D. Paranormal Romance: Christine Feehan's *Dark Prince* (1999), the first of many titles about a beautiful hunter with ESP captivated by the prince of the Carpathians, and J. R. Ward's *Dark Lover* (2005), the first of many novels in the Black Dagger Brotherhood series

International Paranormal Romance: New Zealand's Nalini Singh, author of *Desert Warrior* (2003), which led to her Psy-Changeling and Guild Hunter series

E. Romance Suspense: Jayne Ann Krentz is author of a string of *New York Times* bestselling romances under seven different pseudonyms that started with *Gentle Pirate* (1979), which was published as a "Candlelight Ecstasy Romance."

8. **Historical:** Fictional stories set against factual backdrops can portray famous figures as fictional characters and can have their own subdivisions like WWII novels and romances. They can be longer, around 150,000 words, and these days many are considered mainstream.

Personal Literary Favorites: E.L. Doctorow's *Ragtime* (1975) and Amy Bloom's *Away* (2008)

International Hits: Mexican novelist Carlos Fuentes's *Terra Nostra* (1975) and Irish novelist Emma Donoghue's *Pull of the Stars* (2020)

Most Acclaimed: Hilary Mantel's Booker Prize winner *Wolf Hall* (2009) and Anthony Doerr's Pulitzer Prize–winning *All the Light We Cannot See* (2014)

Best Screen Adaptation: Winston Graham's *Ross Poldark* (1945) led to twelve novels and a 2015 TV saga of Cornish life in the 18th century.

9. **Westerns:** Set in the American West, this kind of fiction employs main characters who are cowboys, ranchers, gunfighters, sheriffs, rangers or frontiersmen. Though it's no longer a big category in itself, it often melds with romance, historical, mainstream and commercial fiction. Publishers of Westerns include Rope and Wire,

Allen and Unwin, Carina and Barking Rain Press, Melange, Black and White, Dusty Saddle Publishing, and Black Horse Westerns.

Classics: *Shane* by Jack Schaefer (1949) and *The Searchers* by Alan Le May (1954)

Screen Hits: Larry McMurtry's *Lonesome Dove* (1985) led to four books and a four-part TV mini-series. Elmore Leonard's four books about US Marshal Raylan Givens, starting with *Pronto* (1993), were made into the great 2010–2015 FX TV series *Justified* (now on Netflix). *Revenant* by Michael Punke (2002), which was made into a 2015 movie, won a best actor Academy Award for Leonardo DiCaprio.

Biggest Romantic Western Hits: Beverly Jenkins, born in Detroit, is the author of *Destiny's Embrace* (2013), *Forbidden* (2016) and *Tempest* (2018), Western romances that focus on 19th century African-American characters.

Feminist Breakthrough: The *New York Times* called *Heresy* by Melissa Lenhardt (2018) an "all out women-driven, queer, trans-gender, multiracial takeover of the old West."

EXPERT ADVICE FROM A MYSTERIOUS AUTHOR

I asked my former student Hilary Davidson to share tips for break-ing into the mystery book category. She's now the bestselling author of seven award-winning crime novels including *The Damage Done* (2010), *Evil in All Its Disguises (*2013) and her latest *Don't Look Down* (2020). Here are her top seven pieces of advice.

1. **Find Where Dead Bodies Are Published:** Like with other fic-tional books, it's smart to get clips in magazines and webzines first, but this is a specialized market. You can sell short mystery, thriller and crime stories to such great titled pubs as *Over My Dead Body*, *Flash Bang, Switchblade, Tough, The Dark City, Noir Nation, Ellery Queen,* and *Alfred Hitchcock Mystery* magazines, *Occult Detective Quarterly*, as well as in anthologies.

2. **Join Your Crime Community:** Check out Mystery Writers of America (MWA), Crime Writers of Color (CWOC), International Thriller Writers (TW), Sisters in Crime (which has a subgroup called Guppies), The Butler Did It crime book club and Mystery Readers International.

3. **Web Stalk:** Read agents' websites very carefully. If they say they specialize in cozy mysteries, they are probably not a good fit for a blood-splattered thriller.

4. **Ask Experts:** Don't lose sleep over whether to call your book crime, mystery, thriller or horror. Sometimes it's an arbitrary marketing decision that your agent or editor will make. "For example, a book by a male author that's called a thriller would be called suspense if the author is female," Davidson explained, commenting (as many do) on publishing's past preference for white male authors.

5. **Be Trendless:** Write what you feel compelled to write. By the time you jump on a trend and your book comes out, it can be over.

6. **Criminal Minds Want to Know:** To get fresh ideas, read newspapers, search archives and LexisNexis, Google police blotters and court records, and ask lawyers, doctors and EMTs about their recent cases.

7. **Characterize Carefully:** "Remember a great mystery is about the people and the forces who made them who they are," said Davidson. "So let your characters guide your story."

SECTION FOUR:
CHILDREN'S LIT

Although many lists of kids' books vary with the names of categories, publishers usually classify kids' books with these divisions:

1. Baby Books (newborn–3)
2. Picture Books (3–8)
3. Easy Readers—Also Called Early Readers, Ez Or Emerging Reader (4–7)
4. Chapter Books or Young Readers (6–9)
5. Middle-Grade Books—MG (8–12)
6. Young Adult—YA (12–18)
7. New Adult—NA (18–30)

CHAPTER 10

Picture Books

HOW *NOT* TO LAUNCH A PICTURE BOOK

1. **Assume since It's So Short It'll Be Simple:** You never had any luck selling your adult novels. But how hard could it be to publish the little ditties your kids love?

2. **Put Together Drawings That Made Your Toddler Laugh:** Write cute captions that tell a story and before getting any feedback, send them to Random House.

3. **Include Your Baby's Photo Montage:** Agents and editors will love to see your adorable little girl. Suggest they use a picture of both of you for the author photo. Don't check to see if picture books use author photos. (They usually don't.)

4. **Submit 100 Pages in Rhyme:** Don't bother to research the regular length of picture book, which is 32 pages, or learn that most are not rhyming.

5. **Tell the Editor Who the Illustrator Must Be:** Though your husband is a lawyer who has no drawing experience, he has a good sense with colors and always wanted to be an artist. So win-win, right?

6. **Cram 300 Words on One Page of Your Board Book:** Ignore the fact that most pages in this category contain 10 words. Yours is special.

7. **Add Instructions for Parents:** If they read it out loud the way you did, their child will enjoy it more. So put footnotes throughout.

8. **Make Your Book for "All Kids":** No matter that a two-year-old can't read and a seven-year-old won't like anything a toddler would. If it's too sophisticated, the parents can just wait a year or two.

9. **Preach and Lecture a Lot:** Forget that little kids don't want to be told what to do and certainly don't want to read a book that sounds like their teachers or parents.

10. **Decide You'll Make a Mint Self-Publishing:** If no agents or editors can see the brilliance of your idea, refuse to acknowledge that you're probably doing something wrong that needs to be fixed. Instead, get it out there quickly yourself and quit your day job, since you're sure to make millions.

GETTING THE RIGHT PICTURE

While picture books are often read to children by their parents and teachers, don't speak directly to adults. Every expert I asked said the biggest mistake aspiring picture-book authors make is to sound preachy, trying too hard to impart heavy-handed wisdom that turns little kids off. Remember, they are your audience. Figuring out how to relate to and amuse new readers—and not lecture, recite rules, or reprimand—is what historically unlocked the entire genre.

The earliest illustrated textbook specifically to entertain children was published in 1658 in Latin and German by Czech educator John Amos Comenius, according to *Encyclopedia Britannica*. His *Orbis Sensualium Pictus*—or *The Visible World in Pictures*—was a visual guide for kids with 150 drawings of animals and people. Using a humorous voice to speak directly to children was a breakthrough that explains why it remained popular in Europe for two centuries. While it contained hidden religious and moral indoctrination, an analysis in *The Public Domain Review* likens the first chapter to an early *Old MacDonald Had a Farm* teaching kids to learn letters and sounds by imitating animal noises: Cats cry out "nau nau" instead of "meow meow," and we learn that "the Duck quacketh" (anas tetrinnit), "the Hare squeaketh" (lapus vagit), and "The Crow crieth" (cornix cornicatur).

A Little Pretty Pocket-Book from 1744 by writer and bookseller John Newbery—considered the father of children's lit—was the first story-book with drawings marketed as pleasure reading to kids in English. To underscore the fun, it was sold with free gifts (a ball for a boy and a pincushion for a girl). The prestigious John Newbery Medal—given by the Association for Library Service to Children annually since 1921—is named after him. Illustrated versions of fairy and folk tales by the Brothers Grimm and Hans Christian Anderson followed, as did Lewis Carroll's *Alice's Adventures in Wonderland* (1866).

My own favorite book growing up was *A Child's Garden of Verses*, published in 1885 by world traveler Robert Louis Stevenson. Born in 1850 in Edinburgh, Scotland, Stevenson dedicated it to "Cummy," his childhood nurse Alison Cunningham, and crafted it as if he were a child writing for other children. The sixty-five funny and engaging poems were unusual for the time in that they often addressed illness, loneliness and depression. Shapiro family lore had it that before the age of two I was marching around my house reciting *My Shadow*: "I have a little shadow that goes in and out with me,/And what can be the use of him is more than I can see." (Let's analyze that.)

Stevenson's parents (like mine) were unhappy he was a writer. He was supposed to be an engineer like his father, then studied to become a lawyer (the profession my father pushed on me). But Stevenson rebelled and became a liberal bohemian. He was best known for his classic novel *Treasure Island* (1883), aimed at readers seven and older. It was his first big success, made into fifty film and TV versions and twenty-four major stage adaptations. Note—even back then getting "clips" was a good way to launch a book—it was serialized in 1881's *Young Folks* magazine, originally titled *The Sea Cook: A Story for Boys*. And illustrated stories for kids from *Ladies Home Journal*, *Good Housekeeping*, *Cosmopolitan* and *Woman's Home Companion* led to longer work too.

Popular early American picture books included Frank L. Baum's *The Wonderful World of Oz* (1900), Beatrix Potter's *The Tale of Peter Rabbit* (1902), Rose O'Neill's *The Kewpies and Dotty Darling* (1912), Johnny Gruelle's *Raggedy Ann Stories* (1920), Wanda Gág's *Millions of Cats* (1928), Dr. Seuss's *And to Think I Saw It on Mulberry Street* (1937), H.A. Ray's *Curious George* (1941), Margaret Wise Brown's *Goodnight Moon (1947)*, Beverly Cleary's *Beezus and Ramona* (1955) and Rosemary Wells's *Noisy Nora* (1973). Wells's *Max and Ruby* and *Timothy Goes to School* books became animated TV shows. Female voices abounded, yet most authors and characters were white.

The first young children's books with Black characters were teacher Evangeline Harris Merriweather's illustrated 1938 primary-grade series *The Family* and *Stories for Little Tots* (1940). Ellen Terry is credited with publishing the initial picture books by a Black author in *Janie Belle* (1940), which had a Black baby on the cover. Found in a garbage can, she is taken to the hospital and saved by a nurse. *My Dog Rinty* (1946) showed a real Black child on the cover holding a dog (who then ran away in the story). Yet *The Snowy Day*, the most successful picture book with Black characters, published in 1962 was by a white Jewish writer/illustrator Ezra Jack Keats and won the 1963 Caldecott Medal. Viking reissued a special 50th anniversary edition.

Lists of modern classics in this genre seem overstuffed with white male authors: *Are You My Mother* by P.D. Eastman (1960), Maurice Sendak's *Where the Wild Things Are* (1963), Shel Silverstein's *The Giving Tree* (1964), Roald Dahl's *Charlie and the Chocolate Factory* (1964) and Dr. Seuss's subsequent bestsellers *Green Eggs and Ham*, *The Cat in the Hat* and *How the Grinch Stole Christmas*—though some have fallen out of favor.

More recently, it has become easier to find books by women from different backgrounds, like Andrea Davis Pinkney's *Pretty Brown Face* (1997), Beverly Blacksheep's *Baby Learns about Colors* (2003), Nancy Tillman's *On the Night You Were Born* (2005), Grace Lin's *Where the Mountain Meets the Moon* (2009), Isabel Quintero's *Ugly Cat and Pablo*

(2017), Sharee Miller's *Don't Touch My Hair* (2018) and Tiffany Rose's *M Is for Melanin: A Celebration of the Black Child* (2019). Personal favorites are by New School alums Bethany Hegedus's *Huddle Up! Cuddle Up!* (Viking, 2020) and *Rise! From Caged Bird to Poet of the People, Maya Angelou* (Lee and Low Books, 2019), along with Renee Watson's Random House picture books *A Place Where Hurricanes Happen* (2010) and *Harlem's Little Blackbird* (2012), which tells the story of Florence Mills, who was born to former slaves and became a famous cabaret singer during the Harlem Renaissance.

Increasingly, picture books are tackling bigger topics. "I've been reading children's books that start conversations about racial injustice, LGBTQ issues and diversity," said children's editor Angie Chen. She mentioned: *Antiracist Baby* (2020) by Ibram X. Kendi, based on his adult bestseller, *I Am Enough* by Grace Byers (2018), *Last Stop on Market Street* by Matt de La Peña (2015) and the *Press Start!*, a series launched in 2017 by Thomas Flintham comprised of fun chapter books for reluctant readers who love video games.

While many kid books by gay authors alluded to same-sex couplings in animals or nature, the first picture book to suggest human gayness was author/illustrator Tomie dePaola's *Oliver Button Is a Sissy* (1979). *Heather Has Two Mommies* by Lesléa Newman and Laura Cornell (1989), which was banned in many schools and libraries, has been recently reissued in a new edition.

The Today Show not long ago highlighted picture books that celebrate gay pride. *Peanut Goes for the Gold* (2020) by Queer Eye's Jonathan Van Ness centers around a gender nonbinary guinea pig with a love of rhythmic gymnastics. *When Aidan Became a Brother* (2019) by transgender author Kyle Lukoff is a groundbreaking book that celebrates the changes in a transgender boy's life. In nonfiction there's *Pride: The Story of Harvey Milk and the Rainbow Flag* by Rob Sanders and Steven Salerno (2018), which commemorates the 40th anniversary of the Rainbow Pride Flag. *It Feels Good to Be Yourself: A Book About Gender Identity* (2019) by Theresa Thorn and Noah Grigni, is a primer on gender identity that defines the terms transgender, cisgender and nonbinary, as well as pronouns.

HERE'S HOW TO GET INTO THE PICTURE

There are different categories of picture books that are referred to by such various titles as: Baby, Board, Concept, Counting, Alphabet, Rhyming, Wordless, Toy, Novelty, Picture, Movable, Popup and Story books, as well as Easy Readers.

If you are a writer and not a known visual artist, keep in mind that most publishers have their own stable of illustrators, said Chen, who has worked in children's books at FSG, Scholastic and Workman Publishing. Unless you have experience doing art or a connection to Roz Chast, just pitch yourself as a writer. And keep an open mind because if you want a mainstream publisher, the decision about who does your cover, designs the type and illustrates your book is probably not yours to make. Don't add too many art notes to the manuscript either. Your job is to focus on the words.

More things to keep in mind: These books tend to revolve around the story of only one character—either a person or an animal. Unless you are a published poet, try not to rhyme, since rhyming books are harder to sell. They can't be translated into foreign languages, which gives them less value to agents and editors. Even a short picture book text needs some kind of conflict to move the story along. Be careful not to be too preachy or heavy-handed with messages which need to be wrapped up in a story that's engaging, funny and relatable. Kids don't like to be told what to do, in real life or in books.

EXPERT ADVICE ON PICTURE BOOKS

I asked my former student Pamela Jane, a fellow Michigan girl, how she managed to publish more than thirty children's books with Houghton Mifflin Harcourt, Harper, Scholastic, Simon and Schuster's Atheneum, Bantam and other top houses. Though she describes herself as "old school," elements of her journey will help younger students trying to fight the odds in current day. "At thirty-eight, I was struggling to sell a book after thousands of rejections," Jane said over the phone. "I took a class on kidlit with a renowned teacher at The New School in 1985. I showed her my story, *Noelle of the Nutcracker*, about a little ballerina who longs to dance in that show but can't.

'Don't write fantasy. Don't write seasonal material. And for heaven's sake, don't write about dolls,' she told me. I was crushed. I was so upset I went home and broke a vase. The teacher wanted me to write a more authentic story of young anguish, like Judy Blume. She didn't know that what I handed in *was* my own story. I'd had botched foot surgery that forced me to quit ballet. I loved my favorite beautiful ballerina doll from my aunt. Then my house burned down and the doll was destroyed. I dreamt the doll came back to me and realized I could make that happen through writing."

Six months later, Pamela Jane sold it to an editor at Houghton Mifflin who didn't change a single word. They paired her with a great artist, Jan Brett. The book came out in 1986 as a hardcover 64-page chapter book in level 4, for fourth graders. It had beautiful black and white illustrations with many other editions since.

Another time, Jane submitted the story *No Way, Winkly Blue!* about a little girl who loved her parakeet, using the name of her real childhood bird. "This isn't a book. I don't think it's even a magazine story," her editor sniffed. Not to be defeated, Jane kept pitching and it wound up a series of six books that earned her more than $50,000 from the smaller Mondo Publishing.

Since everyone I know who sells books in this arena has literary representation, I was surprised to learn that Jane did not use an agent to sell any of her picture books. Her usual advances have been between $3,000 and $5,000, while the illustrators are paid the same amount by the publishers. She admitted that she's pitched a story as many as two hundred times before it sold and continues revising and updating during the pitching process. "If I love a book idea, I never give up on it," she said. Her late husband John was an NYU professor who encouraged her to quit her day job at a law firm to follow her dream to write. To help support them and their only daughter (born in 1994), along with earning advances and royalties on her books, Jane set up many of her own elementary school author visits. Those paid her as much as $2,000 a day, a perk of becoming successful in the children's book market. She was willing to share seven secrets of her success you can emulate.

1. **Read Your Whole Genre:** Jane went to her local library when she was starting out. They had a big children's section and she read "dozens and dozens" of popular picture books for the age she wanted to write.

2. **Dissect the Success Stories:** Taking out a bestselling chapter book, she analyzed and color-coded the introduction, transitions, dialogue, conflict, main plot and secondary plot. She tried to imitate the structure with her own words in her own book.

3. **Be Classy:** Take a class or webinar devoted to children's literature at The New School, Kidlit411.com or *Writer's Digest*. The deadlines and feedback are helpful, as well as meeting like-minded students who are ambitious and motivating.

4. **Join Up:** Become a member of the famed Society of Children's Book Writers and Illustrators (SCBWI), where you can make many contacts and attend their annual conventions.

5. **Start a Criticism Group:** Form a weekly critique workshop with children's authors who can read and critique your early drafts.

6. **Know When to Take Criticism:** Listen to all the feedback from your teachers and fellow students, rereading every sentence they had trouble with to see if it can be improved.

7. **Know When to Ignore Criticism:** While it's good to ask for feedback from experts who have published similar books, also learn when *not* to take somebody's opinion to heart (like the teacher and editor who discouraged Jane from books that later sold big). What works for one teacher, critic, colleague or editor may not work for another. But you often only need one editor to fall in love with your book.

I love these Commandments for Writing Young Children's lit by Ayla Myrick of the Book Editing Associates: https://www.book-editing.com/tips-writing-books-younger-children/

1. It's okay to be different from others, but it's not easy.
2. Bad guys never win.
3. The good guy must come out on top in the end.
4. Extremes rule the world is black or white, not both. Most children ten and under can be quite literal.
5. Characters need strong points *and* weaknesses, even the bad guy.
6. Something can be scary, but it can never touch a little kid's body.
7. Little people can triumph over big people.
8. Poopoo, peepee, tushies, passing gas, burping and underwear are all hilarious.
9. Turn things upside down—as long as they make sense in the first place right side up.
10. Magic can occur as a logical reaction to an action.
11. Regular children can perform extraordinary feats.
12. Regular children can go on implausible missions sanctioned or not by adults in charge.

CHAPTER 11

Middle-Grade

HOW *NOT* TO GET IN THE MIDDLE

1. **Be Vague on the Age of Your Audience:** No matter that a four-year-old, eight-year-old or twelve-year-old reader are all completely different. Ignore all the standards set by children's book authors, parents, teachers, librarians and publishers. They're just stuck in the past.

2. **Add Swear Words and Sexual Innuendos:** Kids these days are smart and can handle graphic language. Just look at YouTube.

3. **Submit the Funny Story You Wrote for Your Preschooler to Middle-Grade Agents:** It helps your daughter get to sleep every night. So don't bother doing more research or revisions.

4. **Avoid Reading Middle-Grade:** You remember devouring *Charlotte's Web* as a tween. Writing your own kids' books will be easy. What else do you need to know?

5. **Use a Scolding Parental Voice:** The younger generation needs good role models to teach them how to be responsible adults. There's enough sly and silly narrators out there.

6. **Add Words You Remember from Decades Ago:** Instead of learning what actual preteens sound like today, sprinkle expressions from your own childhood like "groovy," "golly gee," "jeepers" or "rad." Editors love nostalgia.

7. **Can the Comedy:** Tone down the funny parts. You don't want to overwhelm or confuse literal-minded kids who might not yet have a sophisticated sense of humor.

8. **Be Dumb and Dishonest:** Talk down to kids, creating a fake world to make young readers feel safe, with no strife or pain. They'll grow up to face reality soon enough.

9. **Hand in 350 Pages:** Though most children's books are much shorter, yours will stand out if it's thicker. Don't even bother to double-space.

10. **Center Your MG Book on Adults:** Populate your story with parents, grandparents and teachers who get the last word. This'll give elementary school students a better perspective. Kids know enough about each other. Time to teach them what older people think.

BETTER BETS FOR MIDDLE-GRADE

Also called "tween books," middle-grade usually targets readers between eight and twelve years old who are in third to seventh grade in the American school system. While most are fiction, these books can also be nonfiction.

"This is when kids begin to figure out who they are, whereas Young Adult is more of a completion of that coming-of-age journey," said my agent Samantha Wekstein, who specializes in children's books at Thompson Literary Agency.

"Middle-grade deals with the things kids are going through at those ages: friendship made and lost, family relationship changing, physical changes, a wide range of school experiences, and a growing awareness of the wide world outside of oneself and the injustices it often contains," the executive director of Atheneum Books for Young Readers Reka Simonsen told *Book Riot*.

It always helps to familiarize yourself with greatest hits of the genre you're trying to break into. Famous middle-grade novels through time include Louisa May Alcott's 1868 classic *Little Women*, *The Hardy Boys* (1927), Nancy Drew mysteries (1930), books by Roald Dahl (1953) and Judy Blume, author of the 1970 bestseller *Are You There God? It's Me Margaret,* about a sixth-grade girl who was raised without religion because of her parents' interfaith marriage. Blume followed it with dozens more bestselling books and awards. Lemony Snicket (pen name of Daniel Handler) debuted on the scene in the 1990s with *The Bad Beginning.*

The biggest middle-grade blockbuster ever was J.K. Rowling's 1997 debut *Harry Potter and the Sorcerer's Stone,* which tells the fantastical story of eleven-year-old Harry, who lives with his aunt and uncle after his parents died a decade prior. It was translated into seventy-three languages, on the bestseller list for two years, and led to seven books that were made into eight movies (the last book split into two different films). Jeff Kinney's 2007 graphic novel *Diary of a Wimpy Kid*—a story about a middle school weakling named Greg Hefley based on Kinney's comic strip—led to a series of fifteen books so far and a 2010 animated film.

More recently, Jacqueline Woodson's 2014 middle-grade novel in verse *Brown Girl Dreaming* chronicles what it was like to grow up a Black girl in South Carolina in the 1960s, living with the remnants of Jim Crow. Woodson, author of twenty-one books, has won many Young People's Literature awards. Another much-lauded MG author is Jason Reynolds, whose 2016 award-winning, bestselling middle-grade book *Ghost* tells the story of a Black middle school athlete traumatized by his father's violence towards him, his mother and his four middle school friends. Now a series in box set, they also include *Patina, Lu* and *Sunny.* Other multicultural sensations in this genre include books by the authors Pam Muñoz Ryan, Padma Venkatraman, Veera Hiranandani, Carlos Hernandez, Grace Lin and Linda Sue Park.

"The middle-grade audience is smart and should be portrayed with a lot of humor, heart and respect," according to Wekstein. "The most common mistakes authors make are being too didactic, or making the voice too young or old. You can take on big topics, but you need a lot of sensitivity."

In this genre, the voice of the main character is paramount. While you don't want your hero to be too world-weary or wise, keep in mind this age understands more than your average adult might think. It's hard to strike the right balance. As with most projects, for fiction you have to write the whole book. For nonfiction (like *World In Between*), a proposal will suffice.

GOOD WAYS TO FIND A MIDDLE GROUND

1. **Find Old Favorites:** What were the first books you loved as a tween? Go back and reread them all to see what engaged you. One book critic was so taken going back to her favorite childhood series *The Chronicles of Narnia* by C.S. Lewis that she wrote an entire adult memoir about it.

2. **Know the Genre Now:** If you're serious about breaking into MG, read a dozen VERY RECENT top middle-grade hits similar to your project, before you start writing. That way you'll better understand the kind of voices and stories that sell in the eight- to twelve-year-old market.

3. **Study the Field:** My former student Alyson Gerber, author of the acclaimed middle-grade novels *Braced, Focus* and *Taking Up Space*, highly recommends MFA graduate programs that specialize in children's and young adult literature. She loved the full-time in-person New School graduate program where she developed her first book.

4. **Try Part-Time or Low-Residency Programs:** The growing list of schools for children's lit that you can attend over the summer, part time or online includes Vermont College of Fine Arts, Simmons College, Hamilton, Hamline, Hollins, Chatham, Spalding and Lesley Universities, along with Pine Manor. They can provide guidance, deadlines and connections you wouldn't have on your own.

5. **Find a Mentor:** You can't do books alone. Gerber was lucky to meet Scholastic editor David Levithan at The New School, where he became her teacher, editor and mentor. Bestselling children's

author Renee Watson (author of the MG novel *What Momma Left Me*) was mentored by *Brown Girl Dreaming* author Jacqueline Woodson. In an interview for *Rethinking Schools,* Woodson spoke of the importance of mentorship, telling Watson she's had teachers, parents, neighbors, friends, books and authors inspire her.

6. **Support Children's Books:** Go to readings, in person and online, buy the work of middle-grade authors and post reviews on Amazon and Goodreads. Read the reviews while you're there, to see what readers respond to. Being a good literary citizen will make you a better writer.

7. **Find Online Communities:** There's a very active #kidlit community on Twitter where educators, librarians, authors and agents interact. On Facebook you can "like" and follow The Children's Book Council, Booksgosocial.com, For Children's Sake and other groups that promote reading and writing for kids.

8. **Join Professional Groups:** The Society of Children's Book Writers and Illustrators is an international nonprofit organization with more than twenty-two thousand members in eighty regional chapters. A year-long subscription costs $95. They have bulletins, regional chapters, awards and grants, and annual events that will keep you plugged into the kids' book scene.

9. **Workshop with Kids:** Since you're writing for kids, find out what they're thinking. Watson's books grew out of her work as a "teaching artist," teaching poetry and theatre to children at DreamYard, a Bronx-based youth educational group. She was also a writer in residence at Schools and Self Enhancement, an Oregon-based nonprofit that worked with underprivileged kids in the North Portland area. When Kenan and I were working on *World In Between*, we asked a twelve-year-old daughter of a friend to read it and tell us what she thought. If you don't know any middle-graders, check out YouTube and vlogs and movies for kids that age and listen to middle-grade audio books.

10. **Hire a Middle-Grade Ghost Editor:** After having no luck selling our book, Kenan and I hired an expert middle-grade ghost editor to help us kick it into shape (spending about $1,000). That was our secret weapon and we soon found our agent Samantha and our book editor who paid in the five figures, making our expense way more than worth it. If you can afford it, I highly recommend working with an expert editor behind the scenes.

MIDDLE-GRADE WORDING

Here are tips for the best language choices for middle–grade books, thanks to the *Book Editors* website along with MG authors and editors I spoke with:

1. Choose simple words. For example, "hard" is better than "difficult" or "laborious."
2. Write short sentences with less punctuation, not complicated winding run-ons with overly sophisticated colons and semi-colons.
3. Watch your verbiage. Pick active verbs, not passive. Instead of saying "Many houses were damaged by the storm," try "The storm damaged our house." You don't need to use helper verbs like "he *started* to run," just let him run. If you pick the right verb you won't need adverbs. For example, "He sped" is better than "He drove quickly."
4. Cut long lines about scenery. More interesting are physical descriptions of your characters, from the way they see the world. In *World In Between,* when Kenan was a twelve-year-old refugee, he immediately noticed that his classmates had nicer clothes and fancier sneakers than he did, so we described them in detail.
5. Use less symbolism and more literal, concrete images.
6. Include plenty of action. David Mamet says an audience only cares about three things: Who wants what from whom? What

happens if they don't get it? Why now? This is even more true of young readers.

7. Leave out older knowledge. You want to *show* the hero going through obstacles, not *tell* the reader insights that were learned later on.

8. Try not to flash forward to adulthood or back to the past too much. It's easier to write and read if you stay in the scene in one time frame.

9. Play out all the main action on stage. Don't sum up dramatic things that happened or will happen. Rather than say that parents are already divorced, show scenes of the hero dealing with their family breaking up. (You have a lot of leeway, especially in fiction.)

10. Don't use sex, violence or profanity. Remember the gatekeepers of these books are teachers and parents.

11. Study current kid words; for example: bet, Bucci, lit, YOLO, yeet, squad, dope, salty, Sic/Sick, GOAT, OMG, extra, snatched, Finsta, Flex, highkey and periodt. You can look up the latest slang words, though, of course, double-check that they fit the year your book is set.

12. Create a hero between eight and twelve years old. kids that age don't want to read about people much younger than they are; they'd rather read about someone their own age or slightly older.

13. Focus on their small world, which feels very big to them. Think about their home, neighborhood, school, friends and family— what eight- to twelve-year-olds usually care about.

According to editor Mary Kole's website Kidlit.com, here are the average length breakdowns:
- Young middle-grade word count: 15,000 to 25,000 (64+ pages)
- Middle-grade word count: 25,000 to 45,000 (100+ pages)
- Upper middle-grade word count: 45,000 to 65,000 (160+ pages)
- Middle-grade fantasy word count: 65,000 to 85,000 (180+ pages)
- Young adult word count: 60,000 to 100,000 range (200+ pages)

EXPERT ADVICE FOR MIDDLE-GRADE BOOKS

Bestselling, award-winning author and activist Renée Watson has been so busy I worried she wouldn't have time to speak with her old New School teacher. In the last decade, she's published more than a dozen books like the acclaimed picture book *Harlem's Little Blackbird: The Story of Florence Mills* (2010) and the middle-grade novels *What Momma Left Me* (2010), *Some Places More Than Others* (2019), *Ways to Make Sunshine* (2020) and *Love Is a Revolution* (2021). Her 2017 MG novel *Piecing Me Together*, which Jacqueline Woodson lauded as "elegant, timely and timeless" and John Green called "important and deeply moving," spent months on the *New York Times* bestseller list (twice), won a *Coretta Scott King Award* and *Newbery Honor*, and was optioned by HBO producers from Warner Brothers. Happily, the always-electrifying, hilarious and inspiring Watson made time to offer some advice.

1. **Listen to Kids Carefully:** Teaching seventh graders in the Bronx, Watson asked students questions about how they felt and what they cared about. She eavesdropped in the lunchroom and playground to hear *how* they spoke, what words they used, what made them laugh or get upset, and how they interacted with each other when an adult wasn't around. She also engaged with youth culture, whether it was TV, movies, music or YouTube geared towards eight- to thirteen-year-olds. That helped her to emulate authentic children's voices in her work without talking at them or sounding preachy.

2. **Find Mentors to Follow and Emulate:** To combat isolation, you need a community and writing family. When an editor said her first picture book was too long, Watson read Jacqueline Woodson's *Show Way* and counted the words with her finger. For middle-grade, Watson read fifty similar books and reread her favorites, Sandra Cisneros's *The House on Mango Street* and Woodson's *Feathers*, underlining and earmarking passages, noting the number of chapters and what made her turn the page. In 2015, she was honored to do an event with Woodson, who offered advice, endorsements and

support. Luminaries Nikki Grimes, Rita Williams-Garcia and Meg Medina were also generous when Watson reached out. To pay it forward, Watson founded I Too Arts, a Harlem-based charity that encouraged emerging and marginalized voices, to help young and aspiring authors.

3. **Go Beyond What You Know:** Watson wanted to depict the truth behind the gentrification that followed her from Portland to Brooklyn to Harlem. Along with telling her story, she asked herself bigger questions. How do streets get their names? What determines the racial makeup of a state? How does a liberal city get so segregated? Doing research, she treated her book's settings as one of her characters, exploring the history of a place as well as its people. If you're writing novels and not op-ed pieces, she warned, you need to transcend autobiography and make sure your novels have physicality, drama and tell a riveting story too.

4. **Write What You Needed to Read:** Who is usually left out of the narrative? Who is silenced? What invisible kids never really get to tell their story? Watson not only aspired to originality by depicting smart, dark-skinned Black girls as heroes, she also noticed that most children's books focused on cute, straight, thin, abled white boys. So she made it her mission to write about Black female characters with real bodies. (Alyson Gerber mined medical and mental health subjects like scoliosis and A.D.D. in her middle-grade novels.)

5. **Know the Rules and When to Break Them:** Watson didn't want to follow the typical linear timeline or have a common plot where a slim plucky girl focused on a love interest. Reflecting real life, her heroes had bigger problems to solve, better things to do and didn't need to be defined by a romantic relationship. Reading so many other trailblazing children's authors allowed Watson to determine what kind of storyteller she wanted to be, and whose characters would be in conversation with hers—like Woodson and Lilliam Rivera's.

6. **Pick Your Battles:** The original cover of *What Momma Left Me* had a wide-eyed Black girl with a smile holding up a red velvet cake. Watson felt the facial expression and food were misleading for the complex themes of domestic violence and death. In 2009 there was a controversy over the whitewashing of an early cover of Justine Larbalestier's *Liar,* showing a white girl on the cover, though the main character was African-American. After backlash from the literary community, it was updated to better reflect the story. In 2010, Watson's priority was making sure her cover reflected how she described her hero, a Black girl with dark skin. After she won awards and became a bestseller, a new edition's more apt blue cover showed a Black girl with her eyes closed looking at the stars which conveyed a more serious, but hopeful, tale. For *Piecing Me Together* (2017), Watson requested the famous African-American artist Bryan Collier, who created a gorgeous Black woman's face before a panorama of Portland. With more clout, Watson now advocates for her covers to reflect various skin tones, hair textures and body sizes. In *Some Places More than Others* (2019), she pushed for the Black cover girl to not only to be bigger, but more fashionable, which is why she's wearing a purple parka with matching high tops.

7. **Take Risks—Respectfully:** Watson has pushed the middle-grade envelope with such dramatic themes as domestic violence, matricide, sexual abuse, racism and gentrification. But in order not to traumatize or re-traumatize her readers, she's found ways to be thoughtful and careful, depicting painful scenarios with intention. For example, some of her characters' worst experiences happen off stage, in past tense. In *What Momma Left Me,* Serenity's father kills her mother, but there is no graphic scene of the mother dying. "Adolescence is a time when young people face many changes and often become aware of racism, sexism, violence, abuse, death—in their own homes and their communities," Watson said. "Middle-grade writers shouldn't shy away from the tough topics. But they need to be approached with sensitivity and care."

CHAPTER 12

Young Adult

HOW *NOT* TO DO YOUNG ADULT

1. **Pitch Your YA Novel Before Writing Anything:** Send agents and editors a great 2-page synopsis of your idea. Never mind that to sell a first novel, you have to finish it first.

2. **Propose a Series:** Though you've never published a book, make sure you emphasize that your idea is so awesome it contains multitudes of books. Mention your vision of the billion-dollar film series in the first line too, while you're at it.

3. **Compare It to Blockbusters:** Describe your idea vaguely as "*Twilight* meets *Divergent* with the emotional pull of *The Fault In Our Stars*," forgetting that understatement is better than overstatement and self-praise is a huge turnoff.

4. **Make Your Hero Twenty-Three:** She was once a teenager and you'll do a lot of flashbacks to cover the teenage years. That counts as YA, doesn't it?

5. **Make Your Hero Ten:** He'll be a teenager soon and YA pays better than MG, so why not age him a little lower—so there's room to grow into a series.

6. **Chase Trends:** Instead of following your heart, jump on the latest vampire, zombie or #MeToo bandwagons, not realizing that a book

takes a year or two to come out and by then other things will be trending.

7. **Teach Important Lessons:** Teenagers can be so dumb and self-destructive. Make sure you have one very smart seventeen-year-old character—a class president type—chastising them for smoking, drinking, doing drugs and making bad romantic choices.

8. **Use Your Teenage Diary Verbatim:** You kept such fascinating journals when you were fourteen, you should include 50 or 60 pages unedited. In fact, they're probably a book itself.

9. **Throw in Every Problem You Ever Had:** To come up with authentic teenage conflicts, detail everything about your past eating disorder, addictions, parents' divorce, cutting, depression, horrible breakups, STD and abortion. Don't forget bullying too. YA needs drama these days, so lay it on.

10. **Use Stock Characters:** Create a mean cheerleader, a handsome jock, a misunderstood nerd, a stoner and a loner. Throw in a hooker with a heart of gold while you're at it. When in doubt, re-watch *The Breakfast Club* and mirror that. Forget it was made in 1985 and is completely out of date—some of the greatest themes are eternal.

WISER WAYS TO ENTER THE YOUNG ADULT UNIVERSE

A hot and happening category for the last twenty years has been young adult literature. It's for and about teens from ages twelve to eighteen, though many grownups love these books too. Their main appeal to readers is that they take the teenage world—with its particular problems—very seriously, without condescension, judgment or too many adults weighing in.

Bridging the gap between children's and adult books, YA became so wildly lucrative that famous adult book authors jumped in, everyone from Michael Chabon, Isabel Allende, Dale Peck, Julia Alvarez, T.C. Boyle, Joyce Carol Oates, Francine Prose, Sherman Alexie, Laurence Bergreen, Nick Hornby and Meg Wolitzer, to Louise Erdrich, Meg Cabot and Salman Rushdie. This popularity has been attributed to the rise of e-books, since YA readers grew up in a digital age. Other factors have included the increase of social media, bloggers, crowded BookCon-type (in person and online) events and film/ TV adaptations based on hit book series like *Artemis Fowl, The Witches, Stargirl* and *Love, Simon* books.

YA can encompass nonfiction or such fictional subgenres as realistic coming-of-age stories, fantasy, romance, dystopian, mystery or horror. There's also genre-blending, combining multiple categories in one book like Cassandra Clare's 2007 book *City of Bones*, which is called urban fantasy and combines elements of steampunk and supernatural horror. Paranormal, dystopian and vampire books have also proven successful in this genre, like Stephanie Meyer's *Twilight* (2003), *The Hunger Games* by Suzanne Collins (2008) and Veronica Roth's *Divergent* (2011).

Long before anyone used the label "young adult" there were, of course, many novels with young characters that appealed to both adults and teenagers, like Mark Twain's *The Adventures of Huckleberry Finn* (1898), J.D. Salinger's *Catcher in the Rye* (1951), Harper Lee's *To Kill a Mockingbird* (1960) and Maya Angelou's *I Know Why the Caged Bird Sings* (1969), which chronicles the author's traumas with rape and racism from ages three to sixteen.

The first book by a teenager marketed directly towards teenagers was Susan Eloise Hinton's 1967 debut novel *The Outsiders*. According to the author's website and Wikipedia links, she was an introverted sixteen-year-old high school student when she wrote the story of two rival gangs in her Tulsa, Oklahoma high school: the Greasers and the Socs (Socials). She wanted to empathize with the Greasers. "Someone should tell their side of the story, and maybe people would understand them and wouldn't be so quick to judge," Hinton said. Previous to its 1967 publication, when Hinton was nineteen, there was no young adult market. She'd been influenced by such movies about teenage angst as *Rebel Without a Cause, West Side Story* and *Splendor in the Grass*, though their intended audience were adults, she told interviewers at the *New York Times* and *The New Yorker*.

The book was published by adult trade imprints of Viking Press and Dell, who suggested she use S.E. Hilton as a byline so it would appeal to both male and female readers. Interestingly, this also worked for Lucy Maud Montgomery (L. M. Montgomery, author of *Anne of Green Gables* 1908) and later Joanne Kathleen Rowling (J. K.), not to mention Jerome David Salinger (J. D).

The Outsiders was not initially a bestseller, but teachers used it in classes. That was when publishers realized there could be a separate market for young adults. The book sold more than 14 million copies, the bestselling YA book of its time. Its popularity was solidified by the hit movie starring Tom Cruise and Matt Dillion, where Hinton had the cameo role of a nurse. Her 1975 book *Rumble Fish* also became a film directed by Francis Ford Coppola. Hinton went on to publish five YA books, two children's books and two adult books.

Remember: most successful authors are not married to one book category. That's certainly been true in my career, and in the case of several talented former students who have thrived in the kidlit market. Abby Sher's foray into this field started when she published a 2006 *New York Times* Modern Love essay about going out on a dinner date in college with an older professor who reminded her of the father she'd lost when she was eleven. "I think you have a young adult voice," said a book editor who read her piece. (Note: When a book editor gives you advice, try it!)

Sher has since published five acclaimed young adult books. These include *Kissing Snowflakes* (Scholastic, 2007), *All the Ways the World Can End* (FSG, 2017) and *Miss You Love You Hate You Bye* (FSG, 2020). She's also coauthored *Sanctuary* with Paola Mendoza (2020, Putnam)— along with the adult memoir *Amen, Amen, Amen* (Scribner, 2010) and nonfiction YA book *Breaking Free: True Stories of Girls Who Escaped Modern Slavery* (B.E.S. Publishing, 2014).

"I think on some level, I'm stuck on trauma from my teenage years, which is what I write about," Sher told me in a recent interview. "For me, YA is about reaching out to hold all those teens as they muddle through. I write about dark subjects—like losing a parent, eating disorders and OCD—in the hope that adults will read it too and open up conversations with their kids about addiction, death, sex, all the hard stuff. Sometimes it's easier to talk about a character going through it all, instead of asking, 'How do you feel about your body?' Sher, now the mother of three kids, says, "They inspire my characters and I steal some of their dialogue."

Watson has also crossed kids' genres. Along with her two picture books, she's author of the middle-grade novel *What Momma Left Me* (Bloomsbury, 2012) and the award-winning YA novels *Piecing Me Together* (Bloomsbury, 2017) and *Some Places More than Others* (Bloomsbury, 2019), as well as several she coauthored. Watson travels around the world as a highly paid speaker for educational events, another big benefit of becoming a headliner in the children's book arena.

EXPERT ADVICE FROM A YOUNG YA EDITOR

Wondering how aspiring young adult authors could best break into this genre, I asked my colleague Angie Chen. She's held jobs at FSG Books for Young Readers, Scholastic, and is now at Workman Publishing, as well as ghost editing many kids' books on the side, helping authors fix problems in their manuscripts so as not to alienate agents and acquisition editors. Here are her suggestions.

1. **Make Stuff Up:** "I've seen many YA novels that rely too heavily on personal experiences," she said. "It's good to get inspiration from your life, but teens today can speak and act differently than the authors, who are older. It can be tricky even for writers in their twenties to capture current high school experiences. Trends and fads change drastically year to year. Use your imagination."

2. **Research Teens and Teen Books:** "I can usually tell if a young adult author knows this world. If not, talk to teens in your life, read YA bestsellers," suggested Chen, along with: "watch lots of movies and TV shows featuring teens on Netflix like *Never Have I*

Ever, which is based on Mindy Kaling's experience growing up as an Indian-American in Boston, or *Dumplin'* and *To All the Boys I've Loved Before,* which both started out as excellent YA books." Even if you're trying a realistic novel, Chen thinks reading everything to immerse yourself in all the YA universes—fantasy, paranormal, sci-fi, thriller, mystery—will give you a better sense of the limitations and leeway of the genre, and what teens are reading, thinking, feeling and obsessing over.

3. **Don't Overdo Teen Speak:** Be careful you don't try so hard to capture a young voice that you cross over into caricature. Don't talk down to your audience trying to relate to them, making them say stringed-together jumbles of slang you found on Urban Dictionary. "You have to finesse your characters' voices so they're believable," Chen warns. "That's dope GOAT gucci sick wicked cool bruh" would sound ridiculous.

4. **Get Clear on Your Hero's Age:** "Is your book about a fifteen-year-old entering high school for the first time? That's a very different story from an eighteen-year-old high school senior looking forward to the summer before college," Chen said, adding, "If your book centers on an older protagonist, it might be marketed more towards adults." She recommends these books in the new adult arena: Casey McQuiston's *Red, White and Blue* (2019), Andrea Bartz's *The Herd* (2020), Colleen Hoover's *Ugly Love* (2014), Abby Gaines's *Married By Mistake* (2007) and Jaime McGuire's *Beautiful Disaster* (2011).

5. **Count Words:** The average YA book is between 50,000 to 80,000 words (200 to 300 pages). If your book is much shorter, lengthen it. If it's much longer, you might need to cut it. Handing an agent 100 pages—or 500—of a young adult manuscript might make it seem like you're not paying attention.

6. **Don't Limit Yourself:** In adult books there are all kinds of genres and stories: romance, historical, thrillers, horror, comedy, crime. The same applies for YA. You can write from a multitude of topics, subjects, experiences, places, emotions, ideas and planets.

According to Chen, the main difference is that your protagonist is younger and has a different emotional focus.

7. **Be Careful with Multi-culture:** YA authors creating characters with different races, religions, backgrounds or disabilities than their own has been an explosive issue in this field. Author Amélie Wen Zhao—an immigrant from China—postponed her Random House YA fantasy novel *Blood Heir* after early readers objected to her depiction of slavery. To avoid problems, you can hire experts to vet your pages and make sure you're not coming across as racist, biased or offensive. "When any author is writing outside their own experience, we want to make sure they've done their homework," Scholastic Press vice president David Levithan told the *New York Times*.

"Reliable and mindful research is key," echoed Chen. "It's really important right now if an author is writing outside their experience. Sensitivity reading isn't about censorship, but rather being respectful to the people, places, cultures and experiences you're writing about. You can hire a sensitivity reader to make your book better.

EXPERT ADVICE FROM A CHILDREN'S GRAPHIC BOOK EDITOR

Growing up in Texas, Andrew Arnold was a jock who played football, baseball and basketball, hiding a secret. In his free time, he was a comic book nerd and fan of Thor, the God of Thunder who used his abilities to protect his homeland of Asgard and the planet Earth. "My dad liked Thor, so maybe I inherited the connection. Thor was caught between two worlds, so I overidentified. I was self-conscious since this was before comics were cool," Arnold recently told me over the phone from Brooklyn, where he writes with his rescue dog Jerry.

After studying liberal arts at Southern University in Texas, Arnold earned his MFA at the Center for Cartoon Studies in Vermont and interned with Marvel Comics. While working different publishing jobs, he launched an award-winning *Adventures in Cartooning* series from

First Second Books, as well as his own picture books like *What's the Matter, Marlo?*

In 2019, he became the founder and editorial director of HarperCollins's graphic books for kids and teens. They publish ten graphic books a year for ages three to eighteen, though many have crossover adult appeal. "As the world is turning more visual, educators are seeing the value in teaching students how to be visually literate," he said. "It's an exciting time for graphic books which are no longer being dismissed as funny comics or superhero stuff. They're now being recognized for their artistic and literary merit." Arnold offered book-writing tips from the standpoint of a graphic author, artist, editor and publisher, including why you don't even need to draw to launch a graphic book.

1. **Know the Classics of the Genre:** It's not just comics about Batman and Superman anymore. To become visually literate in the field, familiarize yourself with the modern touchstones of the format: Art Spiegelman's graphic Holocaust novel *Maus* was serialized in *RAW* in 1980, appeared in book form in 1986, and the second volume won the Pulitzer Prize. *Persepolis* by Marjane Satrapi in 2000 described the author's youth in revolutionary Iran. *American Born Chinese* by Gene Luen Yang, about an Asian immigrant family in the US, was a finalist for the 2006 National Book Award. Alison Bechdel's comic strip *Dykes to Look Out For* led to her book *Fun Home*, which was a GLAAD Media, Stonewall Books, Lambda Literary and NBCC prize-winner (as well as a Broadway musical that won the 2015 Tony Award). Jerry Kraft's 2019 graphic novel about race and diversity, *New Kid*, won the Newbery Medal and Coretta Scott King awards.

2. **Learn the Basics:** Arnold cocreated books with his Center for Cartoon Studies teacher James Sturm, who was also the founder of the National Association of Comics Art Educators. These books serve as text bibles in the field, for kids and adults alike. Titles include *Adventures in Cartooning: How to Turn Your Doodles*

into Comics (2009) and its sequels *Christmas Special* (2012) and *Characters in Action* (2013). *Grypons Aren't So Great* (2015), *Sleepless Knight* (2015), *Ogres Awake* (2016) and *Hocus Pocus* (2017) all followed. The Center also recommends reference material for teachers and students, like Scott McCloud's 1964 *Understanding Comics: The Invisible Art.*

3. **You Don't Need to Finish a Graphic Manuscript:** In any genre, you have to write well to get published. Yet unlike most fiction, you can sell a graphic novel or nonfiction picture book based on a few chapters and proposal with panel descriptions and dialogue. Surprisingly, writers don't necessarily need to draw. About 25 percent of submissions Arnold receives have just the story without the artwork. Like in a lot of children's books, some agents and editors prefer to connect writers with artists.

4. **Get Skilled:** While Arnold was most interested in authoring graphic novels for kids, there are many potential artistic careers where you could make a good living doing what you love. Along with drawing and cartooning, he studied art directing, layout, design and editing, which gave him a broader perspective of possibilities in the book world.

5. **Get Your Foot in the Door:** Along with taking an unpaid internship at Marvel Comics, Arnold worked in several capacities at First Second Books, MacMillan and HarperCollins. Being on the inside allowed him to see every stage of how graphic books get made, as well as where he could fit in and his own work and passion could thrive.

6. **Find Your People:** To be published at a top imprint like HarperAlley, it will help to land a literary agent who specializes in graphic books. Arnold singled out Judy Hansen, the president of Hansen Literary Agency, who started at Kitchen Sink Press, a comic book publishing company that pioneered underground comics. Hansen has handled artists Robert Crumb, Scott McCloud, Kean Soo, Kazu Kibuishi, Hope Larsen, Svetlana Chmakova, Raina Telgemeier and

Gene Luen Yang. Before targeting a publisher, get to know their previous books to make sure your project would fit their audience. There are many graphic companies—some niche—including Dark Horse Comics, DC Entertainment, Marvel, Fantagraphics, Top Cow, Adhouse and Blank Slate Books. Each has their own idiosyncratic style and audience.

7. **Consider Different Publishing Jobs:** As the assistant to the associate publisher of children's books at MacMillan, Arnold worked with the advertising, marketing, sub-rights, editorial, production design and publicity departments. "In the end, books are a business," he said. "So learning the corporate culture behind comics helped me be more savvy in writing, pitching and publishing the most authentic and highest quality books."

SECTION FIVE:
SELLING YOUR BOOK

CHAPTER 13

Figuring Out Genre

GENRE FLUIDITY: HOW LOSING OLD LABELS LEADS TO FUTURE SUCCESS

It's easy to get a prestigious label like "novelist" or "poet" stuck in your head. But remember, there are many kinds of books on the market and most successful authors cross genres. If you're hitting roadblocks selling your project, staying stubbornly wed to an unrealistic dream can lead to frustration, rejection and failure. Wouldn't you rather be open-minded and published?

WHEN RETHINKING YOUR CATEGORY CAN BE REWARDING

While stressing over voice, tense and narrative structure, few aspiring writers realize that their most important choice may be classification. It's not just publishers who decide your audience, book division and section of the bookstore. It's your job to figure this out—and it's not as simple as you think. As a writing teacher, I've seen many students heartbroken when their first attempt at an adult literary novel didn't sell. Yet by switching to middle-grade, young adult, romance or another kind of popular fiction (like MG, YA, crime, fantasy, mystery, inspirational, horror or sci-fi), they had a hit that led to a series, bestsellers and ongoing careers.

For a rough draft, it might be best to follow your original vision. But if that doesn't work, don't give up. Consider taking a class, joining a private criticism workshop, finding a mentor or hiring a ghost editor to give you honest feedback and direction. Although I'm very stubborn, I found career triumphs in malleability—something that can be shaped into something else without breaking or cracking. Sometimes revising your initial plan means a stalled project gets resuscitated into a better form where it can live and thrive.

I learned this when I first wrote an autobiographical comic novel *Overexposed*, about two women switching lives. It was based on a provocative Manhattan friend who married my Michigan brother. Editors said it was funny, but didn't buy it. After six years of rejections, I asked an older colleague to read it and tell me the truth. "You have no imagination whatsoever," she said. "Stop writing fiction. Sisters-in-law are boring. Write about sex. And you write best about people you love."

Walking home crying, I swore at her under my breath. At forty, I felt too young and dull to write my life story. After all, I hadn't survived violence, politics, poverty or war. The women's magazine essays I'd published chronicled my bad breakups and worse substance abuse. Then I revisited funny, revealing first-person nonfiction books on my shelf by Vivian Gornick, Mary Karr and David Sedaris—about their addictions and romantic failures. Turned out, reading the best of what I wanted to write helped me break through and I found nonfiction easier to finish and sell than a novel. I switched my first-person humorous fiction to first-person humorous nonfiction and sold my memoir *Five Men Who Broke My Heart* to a wonderful editor at Random House. It led to seven foreign editions and a TV/film option. Having flexibility saved many future projects too.

Excited out of my brains to finally have a hardcover to my name, I wanted to recreate the experience. I was sure my new memoir *Secrets of a Fix-Up Fanatic*, about setting up thirty marriages and being matched up with my husband, was brilliant. A ghost editor disagreed. "Reading about someone setting up couples is a snooze-fest. I'd rather learn how to meet someone myself."

So I rushed to read tons of recent self-help bestsellers, studying their form. After I added wisdom, interviews, quotes by experts, very specific how-to advice and the subtitle *How to Meet and Marry Your Match*, my beloved Random House editor bought that book too. Feeling like I was on a roll, I tried a memoir called *Lies My Mentors Told Me* that my agent said "isn't commercial."

"Why not?" I asked. "Everybody works and has a mentor."

"Because it's seven profiles of old people, three of them dead."

I was confused, since critics I admired said the book was some of my best work. Luckily, a Seal Press editor agreed. On her advice, I renamed it *Only as Good as Your Word: Writing Lessons from My Favorite Literary Gurus*, wrote a new intro and 2-page coda on how to get your own mentors, and added takeaways to make the manuscript more of a writing guide than a memoir. But I was disappointed having a small publisher. "Focus on the end game," a colleague advised. "Write for love. This book will do good in the world."

A magazine editor who read the book offered me a monthly column paying $1,000 each, which I did for five years, ultimately making more money than my larger advance would have. I was so glad I'd kept an open mind, took my editor's advice and compromised.

Next I tried another memoir, *Unhooked*, coauthored with my addiction specialist, which I modeled after the 1989 bestseller *Love's Executioner and Other Tales of Psychotherapy* by Irvin D. Yalom. The rejections crushed me. Coworkers who read it said it was great. It was time to show it to someone else. To get an expert opinion, I hired an experienced ghost editor. For $500 she said three words that changed my project: "Make it prescriptive," suggesting I turn the first-person memoir into a first-person self-help book. "This again?" I asked, exasperated.

"Reading about a doctor telling you how he helped his patients get over substance abuse is boring," she said. "I want to know how to get over mine. It won't take much work to re-jigger so it's universal and helps people."

I added a new intro, question/answer section after each chapter, more information on the methods the doctor shared with his patients, and changed the subtitle to *Unhooked: How to Quit Anything*. The book sold to Skyhorse Publishing. At first, I was disappointed with the modest advance. Yet going with another small press paid bigger dividends in the long run. Skyhorse did a stellar job with marketing, as well as sold foreign editions in Korea, Mexico and China. Even better, it landed on the *New York Times* bestseller list and brought in royalties.

I thought making memoirs into self-help books was a weird hidden twist that only happened to me. I didn't realize it was a thing! Many other authors turned a washout into a winner this way as well. After publishing a beautiful Modern Love essay about recovering from sexual abuse and learning how to have a satisfying marriage, my former student Laura Zam hoped to sell her memoir on the topic, *My Pleasure Plan*. But after having no luck, she revised her pages to also offer advice to other women, retitling it *The Pleasure Plan: One Woman's Search for Sexual Healing*, morphing from memoirist to self-help guru. It sold to Health Communications Inc. just as it joined with Simon and Schuster, so Zam's debut found an agent, editor and wider audience where she could reach more people.

My protégé Amy Klein also tried selling a memoir. Hers was based on her infertility issues and IVF treatments, which she'd chronicled for the *New York Times*. No bites. Then an agent suggested she add how-to information. "I noticed I was always answering questions about how to survive infertility," Klein told me. "No one who is infertile wants to hear your story—they need help. I wrote a new proposal in two weeks. I took a lot from my memoir but framed it around the infertility process, promising to include interviews with other women and couples, therapists, doctors and scientists." Her rewritten proposal sold for six figures in a competitive auction to Ballantine, who titled the book *The Trying Game: Get Through Fertility Treatment and Get Pregnant Without Losing Your Mind*.

A lot of writers aren't sure what shape to mold their pages into; this dilemma doesn't just apply to nonfiction categories. My colleague Jim Jennewein had no luck selling his coauthored screenplay. Not wanting to give up, he and his writing partner reimagined it as a middle-grade fantasy series called The Rune Warriors Trilogy, which their agent sold to HarperCollins for six figures.

When I tried another memoir, *Speed Shrinking*, about how I became a food addict when my shrink left town, an editor said, "There's already food addiction memoirs published where the author gains or loses 100 pounds. You only gained 12. It's not dramatic. But it's funny. Make it into a comic novel." After reading tons of humorous novels, I made the story crazier. The fictionalized *Speed Shrinking* sold to St. Martin's in a two-book deal, along with *Overexposed*. Waiting and reworking paid off. The publishing world taught me the importance of being patient—and versatile.

HOW TO BE A QUICK CHANGE ARTIST

Sometimes changing genres simply requires updating the title, subtitle and chapter sequence, as well as expanding your mind a little. Two colleagues started with humorous essay collections that sounded like memoirs. They put the pieces in chronological order, brought back recurring characters and issues and called their books *Hypocrite in a Pouffy White Dress: Tales of Growing Up Groovy and Clueless* by Susan Jane Gilman (Grand Central) and *The Reluctant Metrosexual: Dispatches from an Almost Hip Life* by Peter Hyman (Villard). Notice the catchy words "tales" and "dispatches" instead of "essays."

My former student Maria E. Andreu sold poignant essays about being an undocumented immigrant that led to her YA fiction books *The Secret Side of Empty* (Running Press). Alyson Gerber first published a poignant piece revealing she had scoliosis as a teen. She was then able to turn her real-life story into the award-winning middle-grade novel *Braced* (Scholastic). Jeff Henigson was told his pages on surviving cancer as a child were his best work. By focusing on the teenage protagonist, his adult book became the YA memoir *Warhead: The True Story of One Teen Who Almost Saved the World* (Delacorte Press). By paying attention to mentors and the market, their hidden childhood angst became artful books that thrived and helped others, too.

While poetry was my first love, paying my rent and getting in the game was ultimately more important than which bookstore shelf my projects landed on. I ended up falling for nonfiction, which felt just as exciting to me. By listening to experts in the field and experimenting with different forms, I was able to make a living producing work that made me proud. Many scribes don't limit themselves by external categorization, including famous poets and novelists who penned writing advice books like Stephen King, Eudora Welty, Samuel R. Delany, Ray Bradbury, Ursula K. Le Guin, Joyce Carol Oates, Lynda Barry, Annie Dillard, Anne Lamott and Walter Mosley.

Based on advice by her mentors, Jennifer Egan combined short stories into her Pulitzer Prize–winning novel *A Visit from the Goon Squad*. The poet Carol Muske-Dukes wrote novels while Carolyn Forché and Mary Karr came out with award-winning memoirs. John Updike published novels, short stories, art and book criticism, poems and also illustrated some of his *New Yorker* stories.

Even if you can't write and sell the great American novel or a brilliant collection of poetry, you can still be an acclaimed author. Decades of struggle and therapy has taught me that asking for tough criticism and then compromising on genre can lead to luck and a lucrative writing career. And what a joy and privilege it is to be a published author at all.

WAYS TO LAND A BOOK DEAL

There is no one surefire way to sell your manuscript. If you ask twelve debut authors how their projects saw print, they'll probably share thirteen different paths. Often the same writer uses contradictory techniques for varied projects, depending on the news cycle, genre, timing, topic, editor, agent and level of desperation. In the same year, I was commissioned by one publishing house to write a pop culture history through a connection (showing only a few clips), signed a contract for a memoir that took a decade to finish based on the full manuscript to a small press, while selling a coauthored novel with a 50-page proposal to one of the top houses. As Roman philosopher Seneca said, "Luck is what happens when preparation meets opportunity." Here are some ways to make book deals happen.

1. Write a great 250-page manuscript you send to an agent specializing in your genre who sells it to an editor who has you completely rewrite it ten times.

2. Write a great 25-page proposal you send to an agent handling your genre who sells it to an editor who has you write the whole thing and then revise it ten more times.

3. Write a great proposal or manuscript, hire a professional ghost editor who changes everything until it sells with a completely different title/subtitle/genre/focus—but you get your name on a book.

4. Finish a great 250-page manuscript and then, based on an agent's request, write a great 75-page proposal to sell it though you've already written the whole book and find it ridiculous to propose a book that's already written.

5. Be a powerful well-connected editor working for a top publisher who scrawls your concept on a napkin at lunch with a fellow editor who buys it.

6. Have a bestselling book so all you have to do is email your editor a short pitch for your next one.

7. Finish your brilliant PhD dissertation and send it to an academic press who wants to publish ten years of work for $1,000 but says you have to do your own index or hire someone to do it for $1,200.

8. Send your completed manuscript directly to an editor at an indie publishing house open to your genre who offers you $1,000 but says you have to pay for your own cover art and PR person.

9. Submit your completed manuscript to a contest that awards publication to the winner—and win.

10. Self-publish a book that sells so many copies, a mainstream publisher buys and reprints it.

11. Pursue a book packager or producer—a liaison who puts together book projects for publishers—offer your services as an author and take on a project you have little interest in to get the byline.

12. Get hired to coauthor or ghostwrite someone else's story for decent money without your name attached.

13. Get hired to coauthor or ghostwrite someone else's story with your name attached—for hardly any money.

14. Become such a famous (or infamous) politician or celebrity that an agent or editor contacts you to author a book. Then pay a coauthor or ghostwriter to write it for you.

15. Hire a social media expert to help you get 50,000+ Instagram followers which could lead to an Insta-book (like authors @ catccohen, @dailyoverview, and @mister_krisp).

16. Mention in the bio of your social media or publicity that you're working on a book that catches the ear of an agent or editor who wants to see it. Then finish it or hire someone to finish it for you.

17. Publish a great short piece that goes viral, causing an agent or an editor to contact you. Then go back to #1 or #2 to complete a great 250-page manuscript or 25-page proposal you revise ten times, then sell.

18. Write a great book, have it rejected twelve times, send it out twelve times more, revise, update, submit and repeat until you get a yes.

ADAGES THAT INSPIRE ME (WHICH I REPEAT AD NAUSEAM)

1. "I write entirely to find out what I'm thinking."—Joan Didion
2. To approach greatness, write about "the unwritten, the unspoken and the unspeakable."—Arthur Miller
3. "Cream always rises to the top."—John Paul Warren
4. "You can do anything as long as it works."—Eugene Mirman
5. "Try to give pleasure with every sentence."—P. G. Wodehouse
6. "The harder I work, the luckier I get."—Samuel Goldwyn
7. "Lead the least secretive life you can."—Fred Woolverton
8. "Be yourself, everybody else is already taken."—Oscar Wilde
9. "Don't ever attach yourself to a person, place, company, organization or a project. Attach yourself to a mission, calling, a purpose only. That's how you keep your power and your peace."—Erica Williams Simon
10. "Stay away from negative people, they have a problem for every solution."—Albert Einstein
11. "The cure for pain is in the pain."—Rumi
12. "The highest form of wisdom is kindness."—The Talmud
13. "Plumbers don't get plumber's block. Don't be self-indulgent. Get to work. A page a day is a book a year."—Howard Fast
14. "Some say publishing is a business, but it's really a casino." —Dan Menaker
15. "Fall down seven times, stand up eight."—Japanese proverb
16. "Just keep doing it well, someone will notice."—Ruth Gruber

CHAPTER 14

Querying Literary Agents

HOW *NOT* TO TAKE COVER

1. **Stalk Agents on Social Media:** Send friend requests to their private pages, bombard them with DMs about your book project, and leave a ton of comments saying how cute their kids are. That'll get their attention.

2. **Group Email Every Agent You've Ever Heard Of:** Make sure to "cc" them all so they can see that it's a group submission. Competition is good. Gets the blood flowing.

3. **Group Email Several Agents at the Same Agency:** Much easier than looking up each one to see who might be the perfect fit. This way, they can fight over who'll wind up representing you.

4. **Send a 5-Page Detailed Email to Introduce Yourself:** Make jokes about your crazy childhood and extensive psychotherapy even though they have nothing to do with your book project.

5. **Attach Your Resume, Twenty Clips, Social Media Links and Photographs Too:** Agents will want the full picture of who you are, what you look like, and what you've been up to for the last twenty-five years.

6. **Ignore the Agent's Website Directives about How They Prefer to Be Contacted:** Those rules are for people with *far* less talent than you.

7. **Spell the Agent's Name Wrong:** And don't check to see whether "Jerry" uses the pronoun "he," "she" or "they." May be easier to just say "Dear agent" to cover all your bases.

8. **Flub the Spelling and Punctuation:** It's just a cover letter. I mean, it's not getting published or anything.

9. **Start with "Though I've Never Heard of You or Your Agency":** They'll appreciate your honesty.

10. **Be Entitled, Unrealistic and Threatening:** Make sure you follow up a few days later, phoning the agent's office and asking, "So did you get it? Did you read it yet? What do you think? Million-dollar idea, am I right?"

COVERING YOUR BASES BETTER

As Ayesha Pande mentioned in her foreword, being represented by a literary agent is the best way to sell your project to a mainstream book publisher. Yet everyone in the business is different and has their own preference for submissions, often stated clearly on their website. Pay careful attention. Some places ask authors to email just a query letter about their book project first, with no clips, attachments or material. Others want an initial letter, with the first 10 pages of your book pasted in the body of an email, not attached. They often make clear what kinds of fiction or nonfiction they want with lines like, "We do not represent screenplays, poetry, science fiction, or fantasy," so nobody wastes their time.

Although many guides suggest long cover letters to agents, I personally prefer short and sweet. Sometimes insecure authors babble, listing every minor accomplishment they've ever had before even knowing if the agent is open to new submissions or their category. It's more charming to be succinct, not lengthy and tedious. An agent can always say "Tell me more." That's a lot more fun than "Tell me less."

The only elements your first agent letter needs:

1. **Connection:** If somebody they worked with or know recommended them, start there.

2. **Compliment:** Mention a book they've recently sold that you sincerely admire. If you haven't read it, read it. In fact, buy it for good publishing karma.

3. **Clarity:** Say what you want exactly and politely, whether it's an answer, advice, a contact or representation for a particular project.

4. **Description:** Specify your title, subtitle, genre and whether it's your debut book, a follow-up to another project, written alone or coauthored. In two lines, not twenty.

5. **Contact:** Put your name, email and phone where you can be reached. If it would help, attach your Facebook, Twitter or Instagram link. But only if you have tons of followers and no pictures of you playing beer pong naked (unless your book is about naked beer ponging).

6. **Credit:** Mention one interesting line about yourself or who you've written for, and/or attach a great new clip.

Note: If you have zero clips and don't know how to get them, check out my previous guide *The Byline Bible: Get Published in Five Weeks*, which details the quickest way to get published. Often an agent will contact writers after reading a piece they admire in a big newspaper or magazine. For example, New School alum Tiffanie Drayton recently published a powerful op-ed on racism that ran on the front page of the *New York Times* Opinion Section, the topic of her memoir-in-progress. I recommended she send it to a top agent (also named Susan) with the subject heading "Black American Refugee memoir/Sue Shapiro connection" and this concise email:

"Dear Susan, My teacher Sue Shapiro speaks highly of you. I need an agent for my debut memoir *Black American Refugee*, which was excerpted in yesterday's *New York Times*: https://www.nytimes.com/2020/06/12/opinion/sunday/black-america-racism-refugee.html

Thanks for considering." She added her name, email and phone number.

They were on the phone the next day, Tiffanie signed with her days later and her book was sold to Penguin Random House in two weeks. You don't need to go on and on when you've got the goods. The only exception is when an agent specifically asks for lots of info in your first query. Even then, a 5-line bio seems better than five paragraphs. You can guide someone to your Facebook, LinkedIn, Twitter or Instagram accounts which may have a longer bio. (But if it's sloppy, dull or rambling—as many are—I'd clean it up before going to agents.) I would not push an agent towards your blog or the Medium essays you haven't been paid for, unless they became viral sensations. And in that case, agents should be the ones contacting you.

Although I've been an author for two decades, I had the best luck when I kept it brief. In 2020, when I was looking for an agent to sell the middle-grade war memoir *World In Between* I mentioned, coauthored with Bosnian Muslim refugee Kenan Trebinčević, I sent this 7-line query to the same agent above. I reminded her of our mutual friend Gabi, her client. Since she wasn't known for handling children's literature, I asked for a referral, using the subject heading: "Need agent for timely new project *World In Between* /Susan Shapiro." My email read:

Hi Susan

Congrats on your big book sale, which Gabi sent me from Publishers Marketplace. I've recently finished the proposal for the middle-grade memoir "World In Between: A True Refugee story," which I've written with Kenan Trebinčević, my coauthor for The Bosnia List (Penguin 2014). I've attached NY Times, WSJ and Oprah.com pieces on Bosnia List. A former student who is a children's book editor said it would make a timely middle-grade memoir (a category my agent doesn't handle). Let me know if you can think of anyone who might be interested? Thank you! Sue Shapiro

Susan mentioned a fellow agent she admired who was an expert in this arena—Samantha Wekstein. Googling, I read that Samantha represented YA and middle-grade of all stripes, especially stories that deal with "themes of friendship, adventure, or encountering tragedy for the first time." And she was interested in history. Bingo!

Samantha instructed authors to peruse her Twitter page, which she updated regularly with query tips and requests. She asked for a query letter with the first 25 pages of the book or proposal as an attachment sent to her email, putting the word "Query" in the subject line. We did. Kenan and I also tried other agencies, since it was acceptable to multiple-submit a book to many agents. Though once an agent expressed interest, they might request an "Exclusive Read." That meant you only give that agent all of your material for a specific period of time—maybe a few weeks or a month.

Even with a connection, it took Samantha a few months to get back to us—not uncommon. She requested more material on the book, so we sent her the full proposal and more sample pages. She loved it. When we spoke on the phone, we loved her and signed on. I was especially impressed that, now that we were working together, she emailed back quickly, like me, and that she was young and an expert at the children's book market (unlike me). Also, she grew up in the Westchester town where my husband was from (hey, whatever gives you an in). It took her a few more months of going back and forth with great book editors—several who expressed interest in the manuscript—until she emailed us very awesome news: "We got an offer!"

Interestingly, the amazing children's book editor who wound up buying *World In Between* had published the first comp title in my *World In Between* proposal—*It Ain't So Awful Falafel* by Firoozeh Dumas, a book my coauthor and I loved and had connected our project to. Since Dumas's book on being a refugee in America was a runaway hit, mentioning the editor's previous success story had caught her eye. (Also, Dumas's middle-grade book was very successfully marketed as an autobiographical novel, a strategy we were happy to emulate, as our editor suggested.) For me, this underscored the importance of spending time to pick the right comparable titles, to make sure you don't say anything negative while explaining why your book will cover different ground and to show flexibility if exerpts offer you publishing advice. Also the editor was a contact of Samantha's, which proves why you should pick an agent with expertise in your genre.

WAYS TO LOCATE LITERARY REPRESENTATION

1. **Direct Referral:** Sometimes a teacher, ghost editor you hire or a close colleague will say, "Try this agent. Use my name" and give you an agent's contract info. If this happens, only use the words "gave me your email" as in: "My teacher Susan Shapiro GAVE ME YOUR EMAIL." (Not "told me to send you my book so you'll buy it and get me a million-dollar advance" or any other variation.) When I offer a recommendation, I often email the agent I know with a heads up.

2. **Word of Mouth:** Students, critics from my writing workshop and fellow members of several Facebook writers' groups I'm in find leads and land agents by posting, "Anyone know of any great agents or agencies for a first novel?"

3. **Writing Programs:** Most of the MFA programs I've been involved with have evenings devoted to introducing their students to literary agents. Some sponsor special seminars since smart agents know they are bound to find great books percolating there.

4. **Social Media:** If you do a search for "Literary agents" many will come up, offering news, along with @Literary_Agents, a directory of #literaryagents who provide tips on how to submit. Find and follow your dream list of agents you'd love to represent you.

5. **Ask an Author You Know:** If there's anyone you know who has published a book through an agency, you can inquire how they met their agent and if they can recommend anyone. (But don't say "Can I share your agent?" To some people that's like asking, "Can I share your spouse?")

6. **Acknowledgment Pages:** Many authors thank their agents, so check out a recent book you admire in the same genre. (Again—buy it while you're at it, for good publishing vibes.)

7. **Network:** I have many students who met their agents at conferences, pitch slams, classes or panels. (I love to include my favorite agents in most of my publishing events. You can watch several for free on my website, susanshapiro.net.)

8. **Subscribe:** There are many online guides to agents and editors you can pay for, including Publishers Marketplace and *Guide to Literary Agents* 2021.

9. **Poets and Writers Literary Database:** This free list of hundreds of agents that represent poets, fiction writers and creative nonfiction writers has specific details about each one's interests.

10. **The Official Manuscript Wish List:** Check out this great arena (manuscriptwishlist.com) where agents and editors post what they'd most like to see but don't get. Recent inquiries were looking for everything from LGBTQ Black and Middle Eastern authors, to "magical realism, surrealism, cozy fantasy and light fantasy" to "Southern stories" and "beach reads and romcoms."

WHAT TO KNOW ABOUT LITERARY AGENTS

1. **No Fee Up Front:** If an agent asks you for money to read or edit your manuscript, run in the other direction. Agencies take their fee—usually 15 percent nowadays—from your advance *after* they sell your book. Never before. (A ghost editor is a different animal, and some agents do ghost editing as a side hustle. Yet the person officially representing your book should only be paid a percentage from the publisher's advance once it's sold.)

2. **They Are Slow:** A newspaper or magazine editor might get back to you within twenty-four hours, but twenty-four days would be fast for a literary agent. Six months is average. You can follow up politely, but unless it's very timely or "has heat on it," I'd wait a few

months. Books take a long time and many agents are busy pursuing celebrities and *The New Yorker* staff writers who'll earn six-figure advances. Be patient. Or channel your impatience by publishing a great piece in a prominent place to get attention faster, like Tiffanie, who landed her agent the week her impressive clip came out. There's only one better follow-up method than to say "Here's the *New York Times* link to my book excerpt I've just published. Have you had a chance to read the project yet?" and that would be "Here's the link to my *Today Show* appearance."

3. **Simultaneous Submission Is Fine:** No problem querying ten—or a hundred—agents who handle your genre. I was rejected by thirty different agencies before I landed the perfect fit for my first books—with Elizabeth Kaplan, another nice Jewish Michigan girl. Once you agree to work together, they are your only agent, often for everything (foreign rights, film rights, other projects). While I didn't sign a contract (and preferred not to), emails confirming our work together constituted the equivalent of an official agreement (and would stand up in court).

4. **There's a Wide Range:** As in any field, there are all kinds of agents out there. The bigger they are, the higher advances they garner and the harder it is to break in. Of the one thousand literary agencies in the country, some are conglomerates like CAA, ICM, WME and Trident. There are big well-known agencies such as Writers House, Folio, Foundry, Inkwell and Pippin Properties, along with many smaller agencies often named for their founders (Nancy Yost, Irene Goodman, Jean V. Naggar, agents Ryan Harbage and the aforementioned Elizabeth Kaplan) who can get great advances from top houses while providing more hands-on TLC to their clients.

5. **Landing an Agent Doesn't Ensure a Book Deal:** Getting the right agent is great, but it's only one step in the (often long) process of publishing a book. Lots of agents go out with projects that never sell. So try to be hopeful but realistic. As my shrink told me, "If

you have very low expectations, you won't be shocked if it doesn't happen and you'll be pleasantly surprised if it does."

6. **They May Ask You to Keep Revising:** Just because an agent likes your idea or manuscript and wants you to be their client does not mean they think you're ready to rock 'n' roll. Many in the field are former editors who'll ask for extensive rewrites. That's normal. You don't have to do everything they say, but willingness to hear tough criticism and compromise is often the difference between dejection and a book deal.

7. **Agents Are Salespeople and Business Managers:** Many top publishers won't consider an un-agented author. You need an agent to find you a top publisher, negotiate the contract to get you a higher fee than you'd get yourself, pay you what you're owed after their 15 percent commission, and intervene if there are problems with your publisher. You don't need a lawyer or business manager, and an agent may resent the intrusive suggestion that you do.

8. **Present Yourself Professionally**: You are a client, like any other. Even if you consider yourself a bohemian artist or poet, for in-person meetings show up sober, well-groomed and dressed like you would for a job interview. Despite potentially chronicling your drug or alcohol addiction, crimes you committed in the past or mental illness, this is a business and you should act accordingly. Don't spill too much, complain, act out, come off entitled or freak out at rejections—usually a normal part of publishing. Unless you're Justin Bieber, nobody wants to work with an immature headcase. (And even the Beeb cleaned up his act.)

9. **Agents Aren't Your Writing Teacher, Shrink or BFF:** You're better off going to an agent *after* you already have a finished project. Yes, some will hold your hand if they think you'll get a great book deal. Yet I find it better to have close friends, mentors, teachers, writing group members and a therapist to critique my work and assuage worries. The more demands you place on an agent, the less time they'll spend on their job: selling your book.

10. **You Can Fire Them or Be Fired:** If they can't find an editor to bid on your book after numerous tries, or you just don't connect, you can officially give notice that you're ending your working relationship. (Though once they've sold a book for you, they will get a percentage of the royalties, foreign rights and film rights forever.) They can also tell you it's time to move on, leave their agency or die—although in some happy cases you can find someone you'll work with forever.

11. **Show Gratitude:** After an agent has sold my book, I've often sent them flowers, candy or gift certificates (though since it could take six months, I sometimes wait until the first check comes and clears before getting too extravagant). And I thank them in my book's acknowledgments section when there is one, as do most classy authors.

12. **Invite Them to Speak:** Although every agent is different and some are shy, behind-the-scenes types, several I've worked with have been honored to make a speech at the launch of the book they sold, or appear on publishing panels I've moderated. It's especially cool when there's a stipend. (Hey, agents also have to eat.) I often plan events with a new student author, their book editor *and* the agent. When the agent is asked, "What new books do you recommend?" they've generously mentioned the author and book at hand, which makes it a warmer book lovefest for you.

A GREAT AGENT IS SOMEONE WHO

1. Returns your emails.
2. Loves your book project and offers constructive criticism that will help it sell.
3. Has sold similar book projects to good publishers.
4. Sells your book to a good publisher.
5. Offers to sell your next book.

A BAD AGENT IS SOMEONE WHO

1. Tries to charge you money up front for anything. (Run the other way.)
2. Agrees to take you on as a client but doesn't email you back for weeks.
3. Falsely claims they've sold similar books you can't find when Googling.
4. Promises they can get you a six-figure advance before sending your book out.
5. Can't sell your book and ghosts you.

EXPERT ADVICE FOR CONTACTING AN AGENT

"The future of publishing will be messy, but we aren't doomed. We need to be smart, nimble and learn to evolve," said fifteen-year publishing veteran, Donwong Song. He's been a literary agent at Sterling Lord Literistic and now at Howard Morhaim agency. His science-fiction, YA and thriller authors include Sarah Gailey, Max Gladstone, Nino Cipri, Amal El-Mohtar, Scott Lynch, JY Neon Yang, Arkady Martine, Mark Oshiro and Carlos Hernandez. The Brooklynite, a passionate sci-fi reader, woodworker and cook, was formerly an adjunct professor at the University of Portland, an editor at Hachette and a product manager for the e-book startup Zola Books. So he's seen the business from both sides, on the West and the East Coast. Here's his suggestions for how to get—and keep—the attention of a literary agent.

1. **Find the Right Representative:** Go to literary events where you network and meet agents, editors and other bookish people. Read the website for an agent carefully, especially the part where they post very specific info about which genres they cover. Song handles science fiction and fantasy for adults, young adult and middle-grade. In nonfiction, he's open to pop culture, history, essay collections, journalism and food books. And he's particularly interested

in under-represented voices. If you send him a memoir about your Jewish grandmother or a how-to guide for gardening your Connecticut estate, he may feel like you haven't done your homework and delete you.

2. **Research Your Field:** You can see which books are selling for what kind of advances on Publishers Marketplace. It might be worth $25 a month for an extensive database of agents, editors and book deals. You can also sign up for the free, short daily email Publishers Lunch. Along with agency websites, check out the Association of Authors' Representatives (http://aaronline.org/Find), Poets and Writers' Agent database (https://www.pw.org/literary_agents) and Manuscript Wish List website (https://www.manuscriptwishlist.com/find-agentseditors/agent-list/), which has a mailing list you can sign up for, as well as the Twitter hashtag #MSWL. It is surprisingly specific and often weirdly funny, where editors may request "something about cheerleaders. Or YA fiction that takes place in a mall." This month Song said he's open for: "Contemporary horror/thriller focused on the experiences of people of color. YA fantasy that feels grounded in a contemporary setting and focuses on the lives of teens with magical or speculative components. Smart, savvy adult thrillers with a literary voice and crossover appeal. No cops. No sexual violence. Author/illustrator for graphic novels for YA and MG, something fluffy and with a good romance."

3. **Fit Into the Agent's Workflow:** On his website, Song asks writers to email him a cover letter and paste the first 10 pages of their book or proposal in the email. He does not want the whole manuscript, attachments, paper mail or weird physical packages with attention-getting presents sent to him. Nor should you hand him anything at a conference or a panel either. If you do, he will be starting from the position of annoyance, not conducive to a great working relationship.

4. **Complete Your Book or Proposal First:** Don't query literary agencies before you have anything to sell. Proposing a nonfiction

book properly usually requires 5,000 to 20,000 words, said Song. Most sci-fi and fantasy novels are 90,000 to 150,000 words. Young adult books average 70,000 while middle-grade can be shorter, in the 30,000 range. If you're getting impressive clips that go viral, or you appear on TV or a podcast, an agent like Song might approach you first. But it's usually premature to contact an agent after getting press if you don't have a polished draft or proposal ready to submit.

5. **Strike While the Iron Is Hot:** If you're excited about a new clip that went viral related to your book, or appear on a podcast, TV or radio show, now would be a good time to kick your book or your proposal into shape. Stay up all night, work weekends, ask for help from your teacher or writing workshop, or hire a ghost editor to make it happen. But Song does not recommend rushing to hand in mediocre pages—unless you want a mediocre deal.

6. **Carefully Craft Your Cover Email:** Though each agent is different, here's what Song wants in your initial correspondence: your book's title, word length, a short bio, any impressive social media handles and an elevator pitch that reads like the jacket copy of a book. Don't list all the literati you studied with—unless one has offered an advance blurb for your future book cover. While following an agent on Twitter, Facebook, Instagram or LinkedIn can work, don't try too hard by repeating a joke one made on Twitter six months earlier, or send direct messages like "Did you look at my query letter?" If you tag him or tweet at him, he may think you don't have good boundaries and block you. Add "timely submission" if your book is topical. If someone referred you directly, mention it in the email. But an agent might call the name you drop, so don't exaggerate.

7. **Follow Up After Eight Weeks:** When you do, include your material again, with a note that's polite but not impatient. If the agent requests to see more of your work, paste your original cover letter into the first page of your manuscript. Otherwise, after weeks or months, the agent might wonder: Who is this person? Where did

we meet? Song goes to ten conferences a year, as well as participating in industry panels and events. If you make his life easier, he might make yours more exciting by saying yes.

Glossary

Acquisitions Editor: A person working for a publisher who acquires manuscripts and proposals, who makes an offer to buy yours, as well as editing it

Agent: See Literary Agent

Anthology: A book of collected pieces by different authors

Article: A short nonfiction reported piece

ASJA: American Association for Journalists and Authors, a group of about one thousand nonfiction writers I belong to that shares information and presents fun conferences

Audio Book or Audible: The recording of a book read aloud

Author: The writer of a book

Authors Guild: A prestigious organization to help writers with copyright protections and contracts

Author's Note: Lines usually at the beginning of a book explaining if names or dates have been changed or other important info

Authorized Biography: When the subject has cooperated with the author

Autobiographical: True to life

Bestseller Lists: Published books that sell the most, usually listed per week

Biography: The true story of someone's life written in third person

Blog: A written website or web page

Book Advance: Renumeration paid by mainstream publishers to buy your book before it comes out

Book Deal: The contract between an author and editor who will publish their book (often brokered by an agent)

Book Dedication: Usually a few lines at the beginning of a book dedicated it to someone important

Book Doctor: Someone you pay behind the scenes to read an unpublished manuscript who can help you fix it to make it more publishable. Also called "ghost editor" and "developmental editor."

Book Genre: The category of writing a book is classified under

Booklist: An important industry magazine with preview book reviews

Book Proposal: Summary of a nonfiction book manuscript used to sell a nonfiction book, with the title, subtitle, overview, chapter breakdowns, marketing analysis, comp titles and a bio, usually 20–120 pages

Book Proposal Overview: A few pages explaining what the book will be about

Byline: A line in a newspaper, magazine or webzine naming the writer of the piece, sometimes offering a short bio

Chapter Breakdowns: Paragraphs recapping the story that will be told

Clip: A copy of a short published piece

Coauthor: Someone who co-writes a project who usually gets half the money and shares a byline

Coffee Table Book: Usually a big hardcover book with pictures

Commercial: Something meant to sell a lot of copies

Comparative Title (or Comp Title): Books similar to the one you are trying to sell

Confessional Poetry: Verse known for being emotionally revealing

Copyedit: A thorough editing of writing that corrects grammar, spelling and punctuation errors, usually by a copyeditor

Cover Letter: The short letter or email you write to an editor when you are attaching a finished piece

Creative Nonfiction: True-to-life writing that utilizes literary techniques. Also called "literary nonfiction" and "narrative nonfiction."

Deadline Club: The New York chapter of the Society of Professional Journalists, a group that upholds freedom of the press

Developmental Editor: Someone you pay behind the scenes to read an unpublished manuscript who can help you fix it to make it more publishable. Also called "ghost editor," "manuscript analyst" and "book doctor."

Dramatic Arc: A literary term for the engine driving a story

Dystopian Novel: A kind of speculative fiction involving death or dehumanization, the opposite of Utopian

E-Books: Books that are only available online

Editor: Someone at a newspaper, magazine, website or book publisher who determines the content of writing they publish and fixes the prose

Elevator Pitch: The two lines you'd use to describe your story if you were stuck in an elevator with Steven Spielberg. Also called "Hollywood movie pitch."

Errors and Omission Insurance: Insurance writers buy to pay legal costs in case they get sued

Essay: A short nonfiction piece or writing that can be first, second or third person but only humor essays can be fictional

Essay Collection: A book of short essays by the same author

Facebook Author Page: A separate page you can devote to your book on the social media network

Fact Checking: A process of making sure your facts are correct

Fantasy Book: Speculative fiction set in a made-up universe

Feedback: Criticism on your work

Fiction: Writing—usually short stories and novels—that is made up. Don't use the term "fictional novel," which is redundant.

Finding Your Voice: Learning an idiosyncratic way to tell your story that's different than everyone else's

First Person Narrative: A writing style using the word "I" from one character's point of view

Genre Fiction: A publishing term for novels aimed at a specific audience, like romance, Westerns or sci-fi. Usually not considered literary.

Ghost Editor: Someone you pay behind the scenes to read an unpublished manuscript who can help you fix it to make it more publishable. Also called "book doctor," "manuscript analyst" and "developmental editor."

Ghostwriter: Someone you pay behind the scenes to write or revise your work, usually without a byline

Hagiography: A biography that exalts its subject

Historical Novel: Fiction based on stories from a past period of history

Hollywood Movie Pitch: The two lines you'd use to describe your story if you were stuck in an elevator with Steven Spielberg. Also called "elevator pitch."

Humor Book: A funny book that can be fiction, nonfiction or graphic

Indie Press: Small independent publishers who usually don't pay much to writers

Instagram: A popular social media platform of shared pictures and videos

Investigative Journalism: News stories, usually told in third person that involve research

Jewish Book Council: A literary organization I'm in devoted to supporting Jewish literature

Journalism: Reporting of the news in newspapers, magazines, radio or television

Kidlit: A nickname for children's books

Kill Fee: An agreed-up on percentage of the fee you'll be paid if writing is commissioned but not published

Kirkus Reviews: An important industry magazine with preview book reviews

Line Editor: Someone who goes over each line of your work and marks notes to fix any grammar, spelling, punctuation or other mistakes

LinkedIn: Social network for professionals

Library Journal: An important industry magazine with preview book reviews

Literary Agent: Someone who will represent your book proposal or manuscript and sell it to publishers for 10 or 15 percent of your advance and royalties. Don't pay them any money up front.

Literary Journal: A magazine devoted to artistic writing

MFA: Master of fine arts degree where you can study such aspects of creative writing as poetry, fiction, creative nonfiction and kidlit

Manuscript: Pages of a book

Manuscript Analyst: Someone you hire to go over your pages and give you notes on what works and what doesn't. Also called "ghost editor," "developmental editor" and "book doctor."

Manuscript Wish List: A website that lists what specific genre agents and editors are looking for

Middle-Grade: A children's book classification aimed at kids eight to thirteen

Memoir: Your own true life story, usually told in first person

Mystery Novel: A specific fictional genre that focuses on unravelling a mystery or crime

Narrator: The person telling the story

Narrative Nonfiction: A way of writing a true story using literary techniques, also called "creative nonfiction" or "literary nonfiction"

Nonfiction: True-to-life stories

Novel: Book-length fictional prose

Op-Eds: Short opinion pages

Past Tense: A verb tense expression action that already took place

Pathography: A "warts and all" biography focusing on what's wrong with the subject

PEN American Center: An international literary and political organization I'm in that fights for freedom of speech

Personal Essays: Short first-person pieces that tell your own story using "I"

Picture Book: A book with illustrations for young children

Plagiarize: To steal someone else's words without attribution

Platform: Your background showing your expertise

Poetry: Short literary work that focuses on careful language and rhythm

Present Tense: A verb tense expressing action currently happening

Proofreader: Someone who reads through galleys or proofs to correct mistakes and typos

***Publishers Weekly*:** An important industry magazine with preview book reviews

Publishing House: A company in the business of publishing books

Remote Book Events: Readings and book talks only online

Romance: A novel that revolves around a love story

Royalties: The percentage of book sales that authors get after their book earns out its book advance

Science-Fiction: A fictional genre based on scientific or technological advances, often involving space, different planets or time travel

Second-Person Narrative: A narration where the story is told through "you"

Self-Help: A service genre of nonfiction books, usually by experts who assist people

Self-Publishing: A book you publish by yourself, at your own expense

Sensitivity Reader: Readers of different backgrounds you pay to make sure your story is not racist, homophobic, insensitive or politically incorrect

Short Story: A piece of fiction much shorter than a novel, often 10 pages

Social Media: Platforms like Facebook, Instagram and Twitter where you can reach many people quickly

Speculative Fiction: A genre of novel set in a made-up world

Stunt Memoir: A nonfiction book usually made of the author's year-long immersion into some kind of travel or adventure

Subgenre: A book category within a category

Third Person Narrative: A way to narrate a story about someone else not using "I" or "we," but "he," "she" or "they"

Thriller: An exciting, scary genre usually involving crime, death or espionage

TikTok: A social media platform for short videos

Twitter: A social network for microblogging where you post messages under 140 characters

Western Novel: A book usually set in the old American West

Workshopping: The process of bringing in pages for critique

Writer's Block: When you can't write

***Writers Digest*:** A monthly magazine for insider publishing that I write for

Writing Workshop: A group of writers who meet to help each other improve

Young Adult: A book genre for readers who are usually thirteen–nineteen years old.

Acknowledgments

Heartfelt gratitude to: My intrepid Book Bible team of Samantha Wekstein, Tony Lyons, Julie Ganz, Jay Cassell, Kathleen Schmidt, cover artists Ron Agam and Eyal Solomon and IT saviors EB and JT.

Great Editors who said yes: Lynne Polvino, Danielle Perez, Wendy Wolf, Naomi Rosenblatt, Katie Gilligan, Roberta Zeff, Alan Henry, Emma Allen, Holly Baxter, Wayne Hoffman, Brett Krutzsch, Erin Keane, Eli Reyes, Josh Greenman, James Taranto, Adam Kushner, Leigh Newman, Sophia Nguyen, Shelley Emling, Sari Botton, Patia Braithwaite, Richard Eisenberg, Julie Pfitzinger, Meredith Bennett-Smith, Ronit Pinto, Zac Petit, Liel Leibovitz, Amy Jones, Daniel Jones and Lincoln Anderson.

Best Critics: Pamela Appea, Sara-Kate Astrove, Jenny Aurthur, Judy Batalion, Roberta Bernstein, Kimberlee Berlin, Nicole Bokat, Ruth Bonapace, Haig Chahinian, Claire Cannon, Enma Elias, Alice Feiring, Frank Flaherty, Francisco Franklin, Alyson Gerber, Eleanor Goldberg, Jenny Greenberg, Sarah Herrington, Jim Jennewein, Tyler Kelley, Jakki Kerubo, Amy Klein, Lisa Lewis, Caren Lizzner, Aspen Matis, Sharon Messmer, Addie Morfoot, Puloma Mukherjee, Guy Niccoluchi, Tony Powell, Rich Prior, Suzanne Roth, Jen Rudin, Carlos Saavedra, Sybil Sage, Abby Sher, Alexzia Shobe, Stephanie Siu, Gabrielle Selz, David Sobel, Elisabeth Turner, Jeff Vashista, Kate Walter, Tallulah Woitach, Amy Wolfe and Royal Young.

Life-saving Friends, Mentors and Colleagues: Sherry Amatenstein, Nancy Bass, Lexie Bean, Peri Berk, Larry Bergreen, Peter Bloch, Francoise Brodsky, Peter Catapano, Amanda Chan, Bob Cook, Eric Copage, Michael Crawford, Laura Cronk, Joanna Douglas, Tiffanie Drayton, Naomi Firestone-Teeter, Ian Frazier, Deborah Garrison, Danielle Gelfand, Patty Gross, Ryan Harbage, Barbara Hoffert, Katherine Goldstein, Gerry Jonas, Julie Just, Erin Khar, Seth Kugel, Deborah Landau, The Landsmans, Julia Lieblich, Phillip Lopate, Laura Mazer, Stan Mieses, Zibby Owens, Ayesha Pande, Galia Peled, Robert Polito, Saul Pressner, Tom Reiss, Mark Rotella, Jill Rothenberg, Karen Salmansohn, Joseph Salvatore, Grace Schulman, Mike Schwartz, Jessica Seigel, Gary Shapiro, Court Stroud, Sabir Sultan, Jackson Taylor, Kenan and Mirela Trebinčević, Vatsal Thakkar, John Turner, Lori Lynn Turner, Victor Varnado, David Varno, Renée Watson, Nicole Whitaker, Galen Williams, FCW, Yael Yisreali, Laura Zam and Michael Zam.

Favorite Midwest Compatriots: Lisa and Marcia Applebaum, Lolly Auerbach, Laura Berman, Judy Burdick, Arlene and Alli Cohen, Rabbi Jennifer Kaluzny, Tracie Fienman and Miriam Baxter, The Grants, Cindy Frenkel, Michael Hodges, Sally Horvitz, Jon Jordan, Rabbi Joseph Krakoff, Dr. Olaf Kroneman, E.J. Levy, Howard Lyons, Dr. Karl Zakalik, The Mandels, Jill Margolick, Tim Ness, Emery Pence, Sonia Perchikovsky, Ellen Piligian, Brian O'Connor, Karen Sosnick, and Wendy and Sunny Shanker.

Loyal West Coasters: Linda Friedman, Alison Singh Gee, Jody Podolsky, Kathryn Glasgow, Susie Goldsmith, Stacey, Julie and Carlyn Greenwald, Michael Narkunski, Lenny Rohrbacher, Anita Rosenberg, Gary Rubin, Allen Salkin, Cliff Schoenberg, Jane Wald, Zell Williams, Gina Frangello and Tom Zoellner.

Beloved Family: The Brinns, Brownsteins, Carol and LuLu Rubin, Helene Zipper, Sivan Ilan, Molly Jong-Fast and my Eternal Pillars: Jack, Mickey, Brian, Eric and Michael. And the brilliant and amazing CR, my favorite husband.

About the Author

Susan Shapiro, an award-winning writer and professor, is the bestselling author/coauthor of seventeen books her family hates in eight different genres including *Unhooked, The Forgiveness Tour, Five Men Who Broke My Heart, Lighting Up, The Bosnia List* and her inspiring writing guide *The Byline Bible*. She's freelanced for the *NY Times, New York Magazine, Wall Street Journal, Washington Post, Los Angeles Times, Salon, Tablet, Elle, Oprah, Wired* and *The New Yorker* online. She lives with her scriptwriter husband in Greenwich Village where she's taught her popular "instant gratification takes too long" courses at The New School, NYU, Columbia University and in private classes and seminars—now online. You can follow her on Twitter at @susanshapironet and Instagram at @Profsue123.

Index

Acquisitions Editor, 70, 170, 202
Agent, 50, 74, 113, 130, 134, 156, 188–201
Anthology, 54, 92–102, 202
Article, 31, 32, 39, 50, 133, 202
ASJA, 128, 202
Audio Book or Audible, 87, 160, 202
Author, 14, 107, 142, 202
Authors Guild, 10, 29, 128, 202
Authors Note, 18, 202
Authorized Biography, 27, 30, 202
Autobiographical, 3–23, 114, 180, 192, 202

Bestseller Lists, 5, 58, 86, 158, 163, 182, 202
Biography, 25–37, 54, 99, 202
Blog, 11, 20, 41, 52, 78, 86, 106, 202
Book Advance, 5, 27, 48, 82, 85, 94–96, 98, 104, 130, 195, 203
Book deal, 7, 9, 52, 58, 75, 91, 130–131, 184–186, 195–196, 199, 203
Book dedication, 15, 203
Book doctor, 122, 203
Book Genre, 203
Book Proposal, 50, 203
Book Proposal Overview, 59, 69, 203
Byline, 46, 57–58, 78, 169, 186, 203

Chapter Breakdowns, 49, 54–55, 203

Clip, 9, 52, 77, 104, 109, 142, 149, 188, 195, 200, 203
Coauthor, 7, 17, 43, 54, 59, 77, 169–170, 186, 191–192, 203
Coffee Table Book, 203
Commercial, 7, 9, 116, 133, 141, 203
Comparative Title (or Comp Title), 57–58, 70, 75, 203
Confessional Poetry, 5, 203
Copyedit, 98, 203
Cover Letter, 89, 188–189, 199–200, 203
Creative Nonfiction, 194, 203

Deadline Club, 10, 204
Developmental Editor, 122, 204
Dramatic Arc, 204
Dystopian Novel, 120, 138, 140, 168, 204

E-Books, 54, 130, 132, 168, 204
Editor, 50–51, 74, 89, 204
Elevator Pitch, 15, 200, 204
Errors and Omissions Insurance, 29, 204
Essay, 71–75, 204
Essay Collection, 71–76, 204

Facebook Author Page, 204
Fact Checking, 16, 20, 39, 204
Fantasy Book, 140, 204
Feedback, 12, 71–73, 122, 154, 204
Fiction, 32, 91, 113, 116, 132, 204

Finding Your Voice, 204
First-Person Narrative, 3–5, 43, 123, 126–127, 204

Genre Fiction, 132–143, 205
Ghost Editor, 12, 57, 71, 122, 131, 135, 161, 180–181, 185, 193–194, 200, 205
Ghostwriter, 5, 186, 205

Hagiography, 25, 27–28, 205
Historical Novel, 141, 205
Hollywood Movie Pitch, 15, 205
Humor book, 97, 103–107, 205

Indie Press, 7, 33, 86, 96, 185, 205
Instagram, 11, 23, 42, 47, 77, 86, 87, 109, 130, 186, 190, 191, 200, 205
Investigative Journalism, 54, 205

Jewish Book Council, 10, 205
Journalism, 109, 114, 198, 205

Kidlit, 153, 154, 160, 162, 169, 205
Kill Fee, 205

Line Editor, 205
LinkedIn, 11, 42, 191, 200, 205
Literary Agent, 4, 50, 76, 93, 96–97, 101, 103, 122, 128–129, 174, 188–201, 206
Literary Journal, 72, 130–131, 206

MFA, 7, 8, 12, 71, 89, 128, 159, 172, 193, 206
Manuscript, 50, 52, 103, 174, 184–186, 206
Manuscript Analyst, 206
Manuscript Wish List, 194, 199, 206
Memoir, 3–23, 25, 206
Middle-Grade, 58–60, 65, 74, 116, 135, 156–165, 183, 191–192, 206
Misery Memoir, 6
Mystery Novel, 135–136, 142, 206

Narrator, 65, 119–120, 206
Narrative Nonfiction, 36, 206
Nonfiction, 18, 49, 68, 206
Novel, 114–123, 127–131, 138–142, 206

Op-Eds, 11, 41, 47, 49, 57, 164, 190, 206

Past Tense, 123, 126, 206
Pathography, 6, 28, 206
PEN American Center, 10, 88, 128, 206
Personal Essays, 4, 206
Picture Book, 147–155, 163, 206
Plagiarize, 4, 25, 39, 206
Platform, 31, 36, 40–41, 75–77, 92, 206
Poetry, 81–90, 206
Present Tense, 126–127, 207
Proofreader, 98, 207
Publishers Weekly, 58, 73, 95, 207
Publishing House, 184–185, 207

Remote Book Events, 207
Romance, 116, 133–134, 140–141, 171, 179, 207
Royalties, 5, 33, 77, 84, 95–96, 128, 154, 182, 197, 207

Science-Fiction, 116, 134, 138–139, 198, 207
Second-Person Narrative, 126, 207
Self-Help, 5, 7, 39–41, 44–48, 54, 98, 133, 181–182, 207
Self-Publishing, 109, 115, 148 , 207
Sensitivity Reader, 129, 172, 207
Short Story, 97, 129, 207
Social Media, 11, 13, 16, 41–42, 57–59, 75, 77, 86–87, 102, 106, 168, 186, 188, 193, 207
Speculative Fiction, 134, 138, 140, 207
Stunt Memoir, 13–14, 207
Subgenre, 8, 105, 115, 135–136, 138–140, 168, 207

Third-Person Narrative, 43, 119, 126, 207

Thriller, 116, 120, 132–134, 137–138, 142–143, 171, 198–199, 207

TikTok, 23, 103, 207

Twitter, 11, 23, 41–42, 78, 86–88, 109, 130, 160, 190–192, 199–200, 208

Western Novel, 116, 141–142, 208

Workshopping, 12, 208

Writer's Block, 11, 99, 208

Writer's Digest, 10, 102, 133, 154, 208

Writing Workshop, 12, 44, 71, 94, 122, 131, 193, 200, 208